b7

BIBLIOGRAPHIA

THE MARC FITCH PRIZE
FOR BIBLIOGRAPHY

The medal displays the shield from Dr. Marc Fitch's
Coat of Arms: *Vert, a Chevron between three
Leopards' Faces or.*

On the reverse, in low relief, there is the legend
INSTITUTE OF BIBLIOGRAPHY & TEXTUAL CRITICISM
MARC FITCH PRIZE FOR BIBLIOGRAPHY
THE UNIVERSITY OF LEEDS

The name of the recipient and the year of the award is inscribed upon each medal. The difficulty of accommodating names of greatly varying length and yet preserving the design of the sides of the medal is met by engraving name and date on the outer edge, as is traditional.

Each medal is contained in a case covered in dark green leatherette with the Arms and inscription of the Royal Mint inside the lid.

BIBLIOGRAPHIA

LECTURES 1975–1988
by recipients of
THE MARC FITCH PRIZE
FOR BIBLIOGRAPHY

**Institute of Bibliography and Textual Criticism
University of Leeds**

Edited by

John Horden

LEOPARD'S HEAD PRESS
1992

First published in 1991 by
LEOPARD'S HEAD PRESS LIMITED
2a Polstead Road, Oxford OX2 6TN

ISBN 0 904920 21 6

*The publication of this volume has been
assisted by a grant from the
Marc Fitch Fund,
which is gratefully acknowledged.*

Typeset by Denham House, Yapton, West Sussex
and printed in Great Britain by
Blackmore Press, Longmead, Shaftesbury, Dorset

Contents

List of Illustrations

Preface

The lectures collected here are by the recipients of the Marc Fitch Prize for Bibliography. With one exception, that of Professor Neill, which is explained in the Introduction, all those who have received the Prize since its inauguration in 1975 are represented. Again with one exception similarly noticed in the Introduction, that of Professor Todd, each lecture was delivered as the address expected of the recipient on the occasion of the presentation of the Prize medal.

Each of the recipients of the Prize kindly agreed to this publication of the text of his lecture, and all of them, with the exception of Professor Shackleton, whose untimely death prevented it, took the opportunity of revising their words though without bringing their lectures up to date. In providing a typescript most of them excluded the expressions of thanks and of pleasure in the occasion with which each of them prefaced his remarks. It has seemed appropriate, therefore, that these preliminaries should be omitted throughout. Otherwise, I have thought it proper in the circumstances to use the very minimum of editorial intervention, and some small inconsistencies which may be noticed in the methods of presentation remain by authorial request.

I am grateful to Mrs Howard Nixon for providing both the photograph of her late husband and the biographical paragraph about him. I am similarly indebted to Mr Giles Barber, literary executor to Professor Shackleton, for a copy of Professor Shackleton's manuscript, for the trouble he has taken in finding a suitable photograph, and for composing the biographical note. In that connection I must especially thank Miss Jacqueline van Bavel, of the University of Stirling, who very kindly accepted the far from simple task of producing a typed transcription of Professor Shackleton's manuscript. I offer my thanks to the Prizemen for their ready cooperation, and to Mr Roy Stephens of the Leopard's Head Press for the care he has given to the production of this volume.

JOHN HORDEN

Introduction

THE MARC FITCH PRIZE FOR BIBLIOGRAPHY

The Marc Fitch Prize for Bibliography in the Institute of Bibliography and Textual Criticism of the University of Leeds was inaugurated in 1975. It is awarded primarily for distinguished work in bibliography. But it may also be given to persons eminent in related fields of study or who have made a significant contribution toward enhancing the dignity of the printed word. The Prize is a gold medal. The winner is invited to the University to receive it in a formal ceremony and to deliver an address.

The Prize is awarded by the Senate of the University on the recommendation of a Committee consisting of the Director of the Institute of Bibliography and Textual Criticism (Chairman), the Chairman of the School of English, a Professor of English Literature, and one member designated by the Donor. Initially the Prize was to be awarded annually, but in 1981 the University decided that it should become a biennial event alternating with the Cecil Oldman Memorial Lecture in Bibliography and Textual Criticism (similarly an endowment within the Institute). In the event of the Committee's deciding that no suitable recipient is available the award can be withheld, but the Committee also has the power, in exceptional circumstances, to award the Prize twice in one year.

The Prize was established through the generosity of Dr Marc Fitch CBE, and it was offered to the University to mark the association of his family with the Worshipful Company of Clothworkers of the City of London (which has close links with the University), in celebration of the Centenary of the University, and to encourage the work of the Institute of Bibliography and Textual Criticism.

Through the good offices of Garter King of Arms (Sir Anthony Wagner) and Dr Francis W. Steer, Maltravers Herald Extraordinary, the medal which I had designed was struck at the Royal Mint. The late Francis Steer was, at this time, an honorary lecturer in the Institute, and also a member of the Council of Management of the

Marc Fitch Fund. It was he who drew the attention of Dr Fitch to my, by then, long search for the funding of a prize for bibliography. Fifty medals were struck, and as a token of their donation to the University one of them was presented by Dr Fitch to the Vice-Chancellor (The Rt Hon. the Lord Boyle of Handsworth) before a specially invited gathering in the Chancellor's room of the University on 21 October 1975.

That date has an additional significance, and a brief historical digression is necessary. My appointment at Leeds in 1965 was in order to realise plans I had made some years previously for an institute of advanced bibliographical study. These included seeking the complementary endowments of an annual lecture and a prize for bibliography. Through the generosity of an anonymous donor the first came into being in 1971 as the Cecil Oldman Memorial Lecture in Bibliography and Textual Criticism.

The Cecil Oldman Memorial Lecturer for 1975 was Professor William B. Todd of the University of Texas at Austin, whose lecture was delivered on 21 October of that year. The lecture came later in the day on which Dr Fitch had made the presentation in the Chancellor's room. At the dinner given afterwards by the University for the lecturer and other guests the Vice-Chancellor spontaneously presented the first Marc Fitch Prize medal to Professor Todd. Professor Todd thus had the unique experience of receiving the silver medal that accompanies the Cecil Oldman Lectureship and the gold medal of the Marc Fitch Prize within an hour or so of each other. It was a richly deserved double, but one not likely to be repeated. Professor Todd's address was given, therefore, in his capacity of Cecil Oldman Memorial Lecturer and not as Fitch Prizeman. But to link his address with the award of the Prize has seemed so in keeping with the spirit of the occasion that, with Professor Todd's agreement, the lecture has been included here.

One other year of award calls for comment. This was 1979–1980, when the Prize, as permitted by the regulations, was awarded twice: to Professor Desmond Neill of the University of Toronto, and to me.

Professor Neill's lecture, ' "Courtesy of the Trade": an Aspect of Anglo-American Publishing in the Nineteenth Century', was announced for 21 October 1980. Regrettably, he had to cancel the visit because of illness. Although Professor Neill was, of course, invited to visit Leeds on another occasion and, later, to supply a text for this volume, he was unable to do so.

Shortly before the award to Professor Neill had been proposed to the Senate, there had apparently been another meeting of the Fitch Prize Committee. As Director of the Institute, I was ex officio Chairman of the Committee, but that meeting was held without my knowledge, though with additional members, including the Vice-Chancellor, being co-opted for the occasion. In October 1979 the Senate approved their generous recommendation of an additional award to me.

The endowment of the Marc Fitch Prize is a most significant encouragement to bibliographical scholarship. I know that all those who have been honoured by this award wish me to record our warmest thanks to Dr Fitch.

JOHN HORDEN

University of Stiring
1991

List of Recipients

THE MARC FITCH PRIZE FOR BIBLIOGRAPHY

1975–76: William B. Todd.

1976–77: Bent Juel-Jensen.

1977–78: Howard M. Nixon.

1978–79: Bernhard Fabian.

1979–80: Desmond Neill.

1979–80: John Horden.

1980–81: James B. Misenheimer, Jnr.

1983–84: R. C. Latham.

1985–86: Robert Shackleton.

1988–89: D. F. McKenzie.

WILLIAM B. TODD, PhD (*honoris causa*) University of Chicago, LHD (*honoris causa*) Lehigh University, is now Kerr Centennial Professor Emeritus in English History and Culture, University of Texas at Austin. In Britain he has been Lyell Reader in Bibliography and Visiting Fellow of All Souls College, Oxford (1969–70); Cecil Oldman Memorial Lecturer at Leeds (1975); and President of the Private Libraries Association in London (1983–85). The subjects of his numerous bibliographical and editorial studies range from the Gutenberg Bible to Richard Nixon's White House Transcripts. At present Professor Todd is engaged upon a bibliography of Sir Walter Scott.

Editing Adam Smith and Edmund Burke:
some preliminary considerations

WILLIAM B. TODD

In his magisterial *History of Civilization in England* Henry Thomas Buckle acclaims Adam Smith's *Wealth of Nations* as 'probably the most important book that has ever been written, and . . . certainly the most valuable contribution ever made by a single man towards establishing the principles on which government should be based'.[1] Somewhat later, on further contemplation of this extraordinary treatise, Buckle roundly declares, 'Well may it be said of Adam Smith, and said too without fear of contradiction, that this solitary Scotchman has, by the publication of one single work, contributed more towards the happiness of man, than has been effected by the united abilities of all the statesmen and legislators of whom history has preserved an authentic account'. Whether we can now accept unconditionally these high Victorian judgments of Smith, or whether indeed his book has in fact moved our present governments now to settle us all in a state of fiscal felicity, it is not for me to say. I cite H. T. Buckle only to demonstrate that even the most learned commentary, here heavily buttressed with some one thousand eight hundred and ninety-three footnotes, has its authority appreciably diminished when it rests, at random, on various unreliable texts. For Adam Smith the author's choice is a late 1839 Edinburgh edition and, for Edmund Burke, another author greatly praised, the copy is even worse: a pirated edition of 1841.

1. The following remarks anticipated the issue of two editions since published by the Clarendon Press: Adam Smith, *An Inquiry into the Nature and Causes of the Wealth of Nations* (1976) and Edmund Burke, *The Writings and Speeches* (1981 and continuing). Though the work now done does not always exhibit, in every essential, the editorial perspectives here discussed, these have been allowed to remain, unaltered, as reflecting a certain approach defined in 1975. As admitted at this earlier date, in the concluding paragraph, attitudes firmly held at one time are still subject to the force of later circumstance.

Though examples of editorial malfeasance could be cited endlessly, I will mention only one other, and this only because the chance selection of texts now operates even more to Smith's disadvantage. Perhaps the most glorious monument to our civilisation, certainly so in its articulation of our linguistic attainments, is the *Oxford English Dictionary*, a work only dimly perceived in 1857, the year Buckle's *History* was published. When finally completed the *Dictionary* proceeds as it says on the warrant of 'first-hand evidence', or the provision of one million eight hundred thousand quotations, to define every meaning and, as well, every spelling employed in our language. Yet that 'first-hand evidence' is usually far removed from the authors cited, or from the compositors who first transmitted the sense of these authors and their especial orthography. Here the citations from Burke are taken either from the 1808 or from the 1842 editions, while those from Smith come from one as remote as 1869.

It is of course only a tendency, not an invariable consequence, that the further removed an edition from an author the more debased his text. Undoubtedly since 1949, when Sir Walter Greg first enunciated his theory of copy-text, passing time and diligent effort can only work toward a rectification of literary works now in disrepair. Still it must be acknowledged that two contemporary scholars, though both operating under Gregian principles, may yet produce widely divergent texts, as in the latest editions of Dryden's *The Indian Emperour*. Further, in this post-Gregian age, it is surely preposterous to claim, for the most recent concordance to the greatest author of all, that this exemplifies the 'true text' of Shakespeare, or that all the half-million quotations then given are 'exactly as they appear in Shakespeare'. For that author the 'true text' will ever escape detection, despite persistent bibliographical analysis. For Dryden, too, apparently, there may also be a considerable difference of opinion. And even for Smith and Burke, as I would readily concede at the outset of this discourse, another editor might deviate from the course I would pursue. Even so, given the evidence to be presented here, I am rather confident that the deviation, if any, would not be substantial.

Let me now for a while dismiss Edmund Burke, since my obligation to this writer has hardly begun, and consider first, and at some length, my prior responsibility to Adam Smith. After years of the most careful deliberation the University of Glasgow is about to issue, through the Clarendon Press, Smith's collected works and correspondence. First to appear in 1976, its bicentenary year, is *The Wealth of Nations*, this edited most ably in all its larger concerns by A. S. Skinner of the University of Glasgow and by Roy Campbell of the University of Stirling, and further edited on matters pertaining to text by the present speaker. I am not sure how Smith would regard this division of labour, even though it was designed to be efficient, for the principal editors were at some little distance from each other, both at some further remove from the Press, the Press itself quite apart from the printer (for this work, in London), and all these parties some five thousand and ten statute miles away from the textual editor. Nonetheless, though the geographical element in this enterprise posed some difficulties – especially when parcels from Glasgow marked AIR MAIL/VERY URGENT were dispatched on creeping tramp steamers – the lonely isolation of the textual editor was, I believe, a very real advantage, if only because I had immediately available at Texas all the critical editions from the first through the sixth: an essential circumstance not prevailing elsewhere. The one lacking at the University of Glasgow is the third of 1784, an edition which, as I hope to establish, is the crucial one in the sequence.

After an exhaustive collation checked and rechecked against all the pertinent editions, I was emboldened to say, at the beginning of a section titled 'The Text and Apparatus', that *The Wealth of Nations* was assuredly, even in a bibliographical sense, 'a work of some magnitude and complexity'. Thereafter a series of bibliographical descriptions conveyed, to some degree, the nature of that complexity, representing extensive cancellations in the first two editions, the appearance of errata in all editions through the fourth, and the details of issue as well for the fifth and sixth, this last constituting the first posthumous edition of 1791. Such descriptive accounts, however, do not fully delineate, in the manner Smith would commend, the real magnitude of his printing. A rough count of the type indicates that this runs to some two million three hundred thousand sorts in each of the first two editions, and two million five hundred thousand in each of the next four, or fourteen million six hundred thousand sorts altogether in the six editions under examination – together with another one hundred and fifty thousand for a separate issue of 'Additions and Corrections'. Quite obviously, on this massive scale, we may expect considerable typographical variation throughout, most of it I am sure due to the author's own persistent intervention, at least in the earlier editions, and some of it certainly arising, incidentally, from the compositors' various inclinations.

Measured in another way more suitable for textual analysis, the Glasgow edition of *The Wealth of Nations*, containing some four hundred and thirty thousand words, records below text seven hundred and sixty-five substantive variants, six hundred and twenty-seven of them in the first three editions, where undoubtedly the author is much engaged, and the remaining one hundred and thirty-eight in the subsequent three where, contrary to the views expressed or implied by all previous editors, I would assert that the author is not at all involved. Since these substantives range from the alteration of a single word on up to the provision of entirely new sections and chapters, a total count of seven hundred and sixty-five must therefore be considered merely as the total number of intrusions, not as any aggregate, in the earlier printing, of the continuing and all-pervasive activity of the author. Besides these more significant intrusions, the Glasgow edition also meticulously records, in several schedules following the text, some five thousand three hundred accidental variants, or alterations in the capitalization, spelling, and punctuation of the text, some of which obviously may affect or indeed control the essential meaning of Smith's arguments.

So much then, at least in a quantitative way, on the staggering task confronting the textual editor of this book. It is now incumbent upon me to defend, somewhat more extensively than was practicable in my section on 'The Text and Apparatus', the selection of the basic edition and the relatively few modifications made in that text. At the outset it is well to recall that for *The Wealth of Nations*, as for all of his other writings, Smith employed an amanuensis; hence the manuscript copy submitted to the printer does not necessarily represent the author's idiosyncratic style, his own peculiar habits in the use of accidentals. Subject to one condition, however, it may reasonably be supposed that in the proofing of the first edition, and in the revision of the several editions following, Smith himself directly entered upon the printed page those alterations large and small which he desired to be incorporated in the subsequent issues. It is difficult to speculate otherwise that, with printed copy before him, he would dictate to his scribe (for this book, a certain Alexander Gillies) the alteration of a punctuation mark or the addition of a qualifying phrase. He could indeed write, however laboriously, and his own occasional writing in printed, as well as in earlier manuscript, copy therefore appears, for

Smith, to be the only efficient expedient. Accordingly, but again subject to one condition, the choice of copy-text for the Glasgow edition necessarily shifts from the first printing – the one we would ordinarily accept according to Greg's principle – to the last printing demonstrably under the author's close supervision.

The exceptional condition, we may all agree, pertains to the relationship between Smith and his printer William Strahan, a fellow Scotsman then operating the largest and probably the most efficiently managed establishment in London. Smith's ready dependence upon Strahan and his absolute confidence in the printer's ability to produce exceptional copy is amply attested in various correspondence. In 1760, while preparing the second edition of his *Theory of Moral Sentiments*, Smith wrote to Strahan:

> If there are any typographical errors remaining in the last edition which had escaped me, I hope you will correct them . . . To desire you to read my book over and mark all of the corrections you would wish me to make upon a sheet of paper and send it to me, would, I fear, be giving you too much trouble. If, however, you could induce yourself to take this trouble, you would oblige me greatly; I know how much I shall be benefitted, and I shall at the same time preserve the pretious right of private judgment, for the sake of which our forefathers kicked out the Pope and the Pretender. I believe you to be much more infallible than the Pope, but as I am a Protestant, my conscience makes me scruple to submit to any unscriptural authority.

Doubtless Strahan did exactly what Smith requested of him, then and thereafter, and much to the author's benefit. On this evidence alone I think we may conclude that Smith most fortunately had a printer ever ready to assist him, even on the most trivial matters, but only upon his prior inspection of the alterations then proposed.

Another great Scots writer, David Hume, was also no less dependent upon Strahan, both for the elimination of annoying Scotticisms in his writing and for suggesting numerous corrections as his works passed through the press. On one occasion Hume confesses that he is 'extremely pleasd with the Correctness of this Edition of my philosophical Writings'; later in the same year he indicates that 'I find you corrector than any London Printer whom I have try'd'; still later, in reference to his *History*, he warmly expresses his thanks 'for your

Care, Exactness, Diligence and Dispatch'; and yet again, on the same matter, he accords Strahan the highest compliment:

> As we are drawing near a Conclusion I cannot forbear giving you many and hearty thanks, both for your submitting to so troublesome a Method of printing and for the many useful Corrections you have sent me. I suppose, since the days of Aldus, Reuchlin, and Stevens, there have been no Printers who could have been useful to their Authors in this particular. I shall scarcely ever think of correcting any more . . .

Lastly we may again cite Smith himself, now also writing to Strahan a year before issue of the third edition of his *Wealth of Nations*. 'This Edition will probably see me out and I should therefore chuse to leave it behind me as perfect as I can make it . . . I must correct the press myself and you must, therefor, frank me the sheets as they are printed. I would even rather, than not correct it myself come up to London in the beginning of next winter and attend the Press myself. Remember me to Cadel [the publisher].' After a time in London for the purpose just stated, Smith writes again from Edinburgh, now returning proof 'which, indeed, requires little correction, except in the pointing and not much in that'. Given then, as so often proclaimed, the printer's attention to every detail, as well as his readiness to advise his clients on the improvement of their copy, and given also his authors' ready assent to these improvements, and now further Smith's own declaration that the third edition was as perfect as human fallibility would permit, it ill-becomes us, as Smith's latest editors, to assume a superhuman stance — to regulate, normalize, and in other ways recast for present use this perfected classic of another age. Even in Smith's casual discourse, as in the eighty-four words just quoted, we might well hesitate to correct an inconsistency in spelling (*therefore, therefor*), as well as another obvious misspelling even in the name of a person well-known to him (*Cadel*), or to supply the punctuation marks required in modern composition (commas after *even, myself, pointing*). Evidently Smith and countless other authors of his time did not regard consistency as an ideal, and to impose it now, as is so often done, is a gratuitous affront to the now defenseless writer. As a recent scholar has remarked, 'Normalising to satisfy an editor's instinct for tidiness or to make smooth the way of a reader is ultimately demeaning for the editor and insulting to the reader'. And to that one may readily subtend the earlier remark of Ralph Waldo Emerson that 'a foolish consistency is the hobgoblin of little minds'.

This much I say, this early, primarily as a manifesto of our own editorial activity, and also by way of preface to what still remains to be determined: whether or not the third edition of *The Wealth of Nations* is in fact the last Smith attended at press. For that purpose we may proceed most expeditiously by reviewing each issue and comparing our own treatment of the text with that accorded it by Professor Edwin Cannan, Smith's last and most conscientious editor.

The first edition of 1776, the only one not listed in Strahan's extant printing ledgers, we may still assign to his firm. Like the others it bears his imprint and, further, displays type and paper identical with that used for the second. Some sheets of the first are also occasionally found mixed with the second, a clear indication that all paper and printed stock was held in Strahan's warehouse. Very probably then, as with Gibbon's *Decline and Fall*, published by the same firm just three weeks before, the original issue was of five hundred copies. The second edition, as the ledgers indicate, was also of five hundred; but thereafter, in response to an ever-increasing demand, the issue constantly increases, to one thousand for the third, to one thousand two hundred and fifty for the fourth, to one thousand five hundred for the fifth, and to two thousand for the sixth.

Between the first edition and the second, published in 1778, there are, as Cannan notes, 'a vast number of small differences', several of which he reviews in his Introduction or records in his collation. Altogether, as the Glasgow edition specifies, the number of substantive changes is five hundred and eighty with, additionally, perhaps twice that number of accidentals; but all of these quantitatively are of such little extent that the second edition adds only two pages to the one thousand and ninety-seven of the first. Apart from Smith's understandable uncertainty as to whether the American revolution in 1777–78 should be regarded as a 'present' or 'late' disturbance, and the frequent shifts from 'tear and wear' to the more idiomatic 'wear and tear' (these perhaps at Strahan's suggestion?), all remarked by Cannan along with other changes, the second edition exhibits most frequently a steady modification of statements which earlier went beyond what the circumstance allowed. As Smith later observed concerning one of them, 'The expression was certainly too strong, and had escaped me in the heat of writing'. Among all the proper names – a matter of little concern to Smith, even in reference to his own publisher, as already noted – some desultory correction is made both in this edition and later in the third, mostly perhaps at the printer's suggestion. On questions of economic fact, however – as opposed to 'political arithmetic', again of no concern – the author here is most exact, at one point correcting the final fraction in a multimillion figure from three-quarters to three-fifths (p. 226). Evidently, then, in this the first revision among the printed texts, the author is very solicitous about all the matters, however trivial, which *he* regarded as consequential, and not at all concerned about the orthographical or pointing niceties which others would regard as very momentous.

Between the second and third editions there is a much greater interval, now of six years, and correspondingly a large number of very considerable differences, a few remarked by Smith himself in an 'Advertisement' to this text and others again duly noted by Cannan. Many of these were also conveyed in a separate quarto 'Additions and Corrections' for use with the earlier editions. Altogether they total only sixty-eight substantive intrusions, but that total represents an increment of some twenty-four thousand words. Among common words, again as before, alteration of spelling erratically continues, entering into English form what may be peculiarly Scottish ortho-graphy (e.g. aukward, houshold, intire, otherways), or what may be called old-style English (burthen, chuse, cloaths, compleat, shew), or what were then other acceptable English forms, though now ordinarily preserved only in American usage (center, connection, humor, splendor, etc.). The unusual spelling *antient* is generally retained thus far in the editions and thus also in the Glasgow text. Other peculiar spellings, usually evident only in the third edition and converting all words terminating in *ic* to *ick* (that is, to *publick, pedantick*, etc.) are also maintained in the Glasgow text, even though they are again 'modernised' in subsequent editions. Analogically in defense of this procedure we could cite the example of one of Edmund Burke's attendants at press, who in conformity with that author's practice, also in later editions introduced a final *k* after *c*. Whether the reversion with Smith also represents his custom is doubtful and, in any event, the question is irrelevant given our intention, already announced, to let things stand as the author finally left them.

To say that Smith finally left the text with the third edition is assuredly to discountenance the three editions following and, with very few exceptions, to dismiss all the one hundred and thirty-eight substantives, as well as thousands of accidentals, which they now display. Sustaining such a decision we have, in an 'Advertisement' to the next issue, Smith's immediate, unequivocal declaration 'In this fourth Edition I have made no alterations of any kind'; and confirming that disavowal is Strahan's own record indicating that, whereas rather large charges are made for author's corrections in the preceding editions, none whatever are entered for this. Even Cannan concedes that there are in the fourth only 'a few trifling alterations' and most of these are 'so trifling that they may be misreadings or unauthorised corrections of the printers'. Yet if any new reading here is sustained in the fifth edition Cannan accepts it as confirmed and thus enters it in his text.

Setting aside momentarily the problem of the fifth edition, and its authority if any, we may usefully evaluate the fourth-edition readings in isolation. Rather than judge them myself, as perhaps a prejudiced witness, I asked a professional copy editor to examine the fifty-nine substantives here represented. Of these she considered only thirty-two to be somewhat superior, among them twenty-four cases where, according to modern practice, in dependent phrases after *if* the subjunctive mode denoted by *were* is substituted for the indicative *was*. And since that, I am convinced, is not Smith's mode of expression, we are left then, as possibly his, with eight other slight deviants — eight out of some four hundred and thirty thousand words. The possibility of authorial revision is thus so remote, especially when compared with the thousands of significant entries in the earlier editions, that we must accept Smith at his word, dismiss any charge to the contrary as 'unproved', a good Scottish verdict, and in general refuse any admittance of this text.

A similar judgment must also be rendered for the fifth, the edition Cannan copies simply because, as he says, it was 'the last published in Smith's lifetime'. Here of thirty-one substantive variants my copy editor would prefer only eleven, among them a reading which in the fifth edition reads:

> In the whole interval which separates those two moments [between the womb and the grave], there is scarce perhaps a single *instance* in which any man is so perfectly and completely satisfied with his situation, as to be without any wish of alteration or improvement of any kind. (p. 341)

This quotation is offered as a perfect example of editorial irresponsibility, for the fifth-edition reading *instance*, which the present copy editor and others have singled out as definitely preferable, is one of the many which Cannan was earlier forced to reject as, in his opinion, a 'misprint', here for *instant*. Actually the *OED* will allow the sense of either word, in this context, though *instant* must prevail as the one retained in the earlier editions demonstrably under Smith's supervision. Similarly, whether Cannan does so or not, all other fifth-edition readings here must also be discounted as unauthorised.

If Smith completely disregarded his fourth and fifth editions then we may reasonably infer that he was totally unconcerned with the posthumous sixth, issued in 1791. Nonetheless, as other authors are known to have prepared final revisions published only after their death, among them John Locke and Samuel Richardson, the collation in the Glasgow edition prudently extended this far. Again, in this sixth edition, after rejecting readings adjudged to be indifferent or misprinted, the present copy editor found among the forty-eight substantive variants some fifteen which she regarded as improvements. But again, as with all the others, the differences essentially are stylistic, reflecting once more only the printer's continuing endeavour to perfect the text.

How far Smith's first printers thereafter continued their laudable endeavour to improve the text, according to the standards then prevailing, and how far later printers may then have debased this text, all perhaps unwittingly, are matters beyond our purview. Our only obligation now is to provide sufficient justification for our own treatment of the third-edition text, the last evidently attended by Smith, according to the prescriptions now generally enforced. Obviously, after due consultation with the Clarendon Press, we have cast the entire work in a modern format and in various ways, fully noted, adopted several procedures facilitating the formal presentation of this work. One matter, hitherto unnoticed, is that several of the entries in the Table of Contents are somewhat more extensive than the headings given in the text: a circumstance which, we all agreed, required a revision of the earlier-printed text entries. Also, where Smith was content with only one index, and his most recent editor with two, the present editors have considered it necessary to provide three, along with a 'Table of Corresponding Passages'. These and other facilities, all intended for the convenience of the reader, we believe will be readily acceptable.

As for the text proper, however, some explanation may still be necessary. Doubtless for a work of such magnitude it is impossible for an author, even one so assiduous as Smith, to maintain absolute and complete control over all his material; and we would thus be most negligent in our trust if we failed to apply such controls in those relatively few cases which escaped Smith's notice. Throughout it will be understood that our intent is never to improve the text but only to clarify a sudden ambiguity or to correct a manifest fault. So resolved we have finally determined, after much transatlantic debate, that eight substantive readings are defective and therefore, with due notice, have amended these eight on the warrant of other editions, usually of texts preceding the third, but never, as it happens, from the fifth — the text selected by Professor Cannan. Similarly, after much further debate, we have in fifty-nine other cases altered the accidentals, all as indicated in a separate schedule. Of these sixteen in the third edition are evidently typographical misprints and in most of the others it is quite apparent that the pointing of the original edition better conveys the sense. Four times only do we venture to correct a spelling, despite Smith's inconsistency in such matters, and here always of the same word *conveniences*; for it everywhere appears, both in the text and in Smith's own corrections of an earlier manuscript, that for this one term he consistently preferred *conveniencies*. Even in this respect, however, we have proceeded only on the further authority of the other editions. Hence in all these several particulars we have intervened only when, in our common judgment, it was essential to do so, and then always with the full weight of all available evidence, external as well as internal. I have little doubt, therefore, that both in the determination of the text and in the learned commentary so well provided by Professors Skinner and Campbell, we have met every expectation.

What we may later expect of the Edmund Burke edition, also to be issued by the Clarendon Press, I cannot readily predict. Happily the experience acquired in the editing of Burke's extensive correspondence will be carried over to this new enterprise, since several editors for the one are now involved in the other, among them notably Dr John A. Woods of Leeds University. Fortunately we now also are privileged to have as general director of all editorial activities the services of Dr Paul Langford of Lincoln College, Oxford. Still, even with this grand ministry of all the talents, there are many vexing problems which, however they may be resolved, will leave some readers quite discontent. Among other inexplicables we will never be able to determine satisfactorily Burke's own share in various collaborations — a matter of some dispute even at the time — nor the extent to which his advisors or attendants at press modified, with permission, his effusive language, nor for the speeches especially the authenticity of several versions early printed in forms each radically different from the other, nor the extent of his complicity either in *The Annual Register* or in the interminable reports on Warren Hastings and India.

Even where the canon appears to be fixed and the text in final form, as might easily be supposed in the contemporary *Works*, there are grounds for considerable misgiving, indeed for great apprehension. For Burke's early *Essay towards an Abridgment of the English History* (c.1760) one must immediately resort to the fifth quarto volume, issued posthumously in 1812, but then only out of necessity since that is the first printing of the work in its expanded form. Five of Burke's other, lesser, pieces, however, are not in the *Works*, though all were printed, sometimes more than once, in his lifetime. Three other tracts of greater consequence are included but all taken from the wrong texts: the *Letter to the Sheriffs of Bristol* (1777) from a 'fourth edition' which is actually a reissue of the unrevised first; the *Speech Relative to his Parliamentary Conduct* (1788) from a fifth edition which by that time displays a number of misprints; and the *Letter to a Noble Lord* (1796) from some edition after the third but preceding the twelfth, the last to incorporate further revision undoubtedly by Burke himself. For these pieces, and presumably for others yet untested, the previous choice of text appears to be quite haphazard.

Whatever the method of selection or extent of text, the collected *Works* present still further difficulties which can hardly be discerned, much less overcome. For one, we have no clear indication as to whether Burke was directly involved in the preparation of the first three volumes, the only ones published in his lifetime. Once only, in reference to a single tract, he advises a correspondent that his 'letter to Lord Kenmore is to be found, I think, more correctly than in the first Dublin copy, in the quarto edition of my *Ineptiae*'. But that isolated remark, passed three years after issue of the quarto volume, still expresses some uncertainty, this perhaps because the issue was primarily the endeavour of his solicitous friends Walker King and French Laurence.

Immediately after Burke's death in 1797 these same friends, now acting officially as his literary executors, intrude ever more aggressively first upon his separate and then again upon the collected works. Burke himself four times revised his *Two Letters on the Proposals for Peace*, lastly in a 'tenth edition' issued 11 November 1796. Yet in the 'twelfth', published 24 October the following year, twenty weeks after Burke's death, further revisions belatedly appear, all of which, we may now surmise, are of very doubtful authority. Three weeks later, on issuing Burke's *Third Letter*, the executors candidly admit that they have made 'a humble attempt at supplying the void with some continuing explanation and illustration of the documents . . . In performing with reverential diffidence that duty of friendship', they continue, 'no one sentiment has been attributed to Mr. Burke, which is not most explicitly known, from repeated conversations and from correspondence, to have been entertained by that illustrious man. Some passages from his own private letters, and some letters to him, which he was pleased to commend and to preserve, have been interwoven'. *Interwoven!* Three years later, in 1800, this 'humble' editorial attitude has hardened into an even more arrogant stance. Then, in a tract entitled *Thoughts and Details on Scarcity*, the executors, now under some pressure to explain their conduct, acknowledge further interpolations in this sketch left by Burke. Nonetheless, they say, 'to the reader no apology is due, if the disquisitions thus interwoven may seem a little disproportioned to the summary statements of the original Memorial. Their own intrinsic worth and beauty will be an ample compensation for that slight deformity . . .' Again note the admission of *interweaving* any material considered appropriate. No wonder then, as was remarked at the time, that this author's executors seem to be engaged in 'a manufactory for pamphlets under the *title* of Edmund Burke'.

Should we now, in our own time, be inclined to accept this earlier judgment, we can easily find still further cause for alarm. Ever concerned to present the great man always in the best possible form, as *they* would judge that form, or even better to construct something new, the executors King and Laurence reissued in 1801 the works first collected in 1792, variously re-edited these works again in 1803, and thereafter through 1827 — then thirty years after Burke's death — enlarged the works to twice their original extent. In an Advertisement to the 1803 edition the numerous alterations, at first casually dismissed as 'some slight changes', are finally expressed in terms which can only be regarded, in our present view of correct editorial procedure, as entirely unacceptable. Certain texts and documents have been 'accommodated to each other', or again, we may suppose, *interwoven*; the orthography has been reduced 'to some certain standard', at times according to Burke's practice, they assert, at other times according to 'the best received authorities', all unidentified; various insertions, also never specified, 'have also been made from a quarto copy corrected by Mr. Burke himself' — taken, that is, from the 1792 collected edition — and notes also are supplied from that same authorised source. Yet one such note, on 'that celebrated phrase, "the swinish multitude" ' here acclaimed as definitely by Burke, we must immediately question as obviously not in Burke's style.

Many years after all this lamentable editorial activity, and long after the death of French Laurence and others who had so helpfully mismanaged Burke's literary affairs, Walker King as sole surviving executor still valiantly carried forward according to the procedures first enunciated in 1803. In the introduction to the fourth volume (1822) of the posthumous works (seventh in the continuing quarto series, thirteenth in the octavo format), this elderly editor, now Lord Bishop of Rochester, recalls that among all of Burke's parliamentary labours the authors regarded as 'most interesting and momentous' those concerning Warren Hastings and East India, and that Burke had earnestly requested King to 'collect and arrange those materials, and publish so much of them, as I might judge fit for publication'. Even if such a request was in fact made, a matter now beyond discovery, we are still unprepared to allow this venerable Lord Bishop to judge for us today, among many revolting disclosures in the East Indian affair, what would be most suitable for us to read. Apart from the curious editorial techniques then employed, and already discounted as unacceptable, we may now be increasingly suspicious, in these later posthumous volumes, of an ever-vigilant censor.

Given all these uncertainties, extending for thirty years beyond the death of the Edmund Burke, what may we propose as the guiding principle for the editors now engaged? To all of them I originally suggested that once we had selected in each instance the proper copy-text — here, perhaps, as for Adam Smith, the last edition demonstrably revised by the author — we then incorporate in that edition, from the later texts, any 'manifestly superior reading'. Presumably such a reading, we could argue, must have been proposed by Burke himself when his works were first collected in 1792 or, if not appearing there, then entered by him in his copy of that collection and later transmitted in the reprintings prepared by his energetic executors. Now, however, after reviewing all that these executors have done and misdone, largely according to their own testimony, as just rehearsed here, I am much less sanguine about this simple recommendation. For one thing, what may be regarded as 'manifestly superior' to one editor, as the reading cited for Adam Smith clearly indicates, could be denounced by a second editor as an egregious misprint. For another, in any qualitative judgment of superior readings, we would necessarily have to recognise five diminishing degrees of authenticity: (1) an authority evident, apparent, and acceptable for those works Burke personally revised: (2) an authority somewhat less apparent when, as is more often the case, his friends may have attended the press, either for his separate tracts or the collected works of 1792; (3) only occasionally evident, and then only in some indefinable way, in all the posthumous pieces *interwoven* by the executors in 1797–1800; (4) somewhat conjectural in the works later edited by those executors in 1801 and 1803 when all of the text is somehow *accommodated*, silently, to certain editorial preconceptions; and (5) entirely conjectural in all the other works edited 1812–1827 chiefly by the Bishop of Rochester.

So regarded, we are forced to conclude that, except for the first stage in the textual transmission, where the author is directly involved, the entire corpus of Edmund Burke has been contaminated in ever increasing measure. We must further conclude that, as this contamination proceeds at various times and by diverse editorial dictates, all undisclosed, any later intervention by the author himself – at those times when he is capable of intervening – will ever be a matter of some dispute. Accordingly, I would propose that we reject every later revision, even if 'manifestly superior', and allow in the text only those few readings which correct an obvious error or misstatement of fact. Whether allowed or disallowed, all alterations will of course be entered in the apparatus so that the readers will be continually apprised of the state of this highly variable text.

With this last declaration I should now desist from any further argument and simply concede the probability that, with Burke especially, further study may require some modification of the proposals here advanced. Unlike the edition of Adam Smith, where the relatively uncomplicated textual history has already been assessed, the necessary editorial work performed, and publication now under way, the edition of Edmund Burke still remains, in many respects, a subject for continued discussion. In offering this prolegomena I am therefore primarily concerned that this discussion should continue until it eventuates, finally, in an edition all can accept as the best that can be attained in these peculiar circumstances.

BENT JUEL-JENSEN is now an Emeritus Fellow of St Cross College, Oxford, Emeritus University Medical Officer, and Honorary Consultant Physician. Apart from contributions to monographs and numerous medical papers, he has written a bibliography of the early editions of Michael Drayton in the second edition of the Shakespeare Head *Drayton*, and has just revised his bibliography of the early editions of Sir Philip Sidney, now published in *Sir Philip Sidney: an Anthology of Modern Criticism*. He has compiled shorter bibliographies of Sir Hugh Platt and John Hamilton Reynolds, and has written on various aspects of book collecting, Ethiopian manuscripts, and Aksumite coinage.

A bookman in the land of Prester John

BENT JUEL-JENSEN

Edward Ullendorff, the distinguished linguist, once rebuked me for using the term 'obscure' about the field of Ethiopic manuscripts. He said, rightly, that scholars since the time of Ludolf have written extensively about Ethiopic literature. However, the Ethiopian manuscript as an object is relatively neglected, some notable exceptions notwithstanding[1] and despite the brief mention of palaeographic characteristics throughout the centuries in the catalogues of the great national collections. Although there are admirable catalogues of Ethiopic MSS in many English and European collections, there are few accounts of the contents of libraries in Ethiopia itself.[2] The following touches briefly on some aspect of the 'Book in Ethiopia', literally and metaphorically, as seen through the eyes of a member of the 1974 Oxford University Expedition to Ethiopia. Why Ethiopia? Some of us had for a long time been interested in the Eastern Churches and their rich artistic heritage. The Orthodox Ethiopian Church seemed still to preserve features that had disappeared in the West with the Middle Ages, not least the continuing use of manuscripts. The marvellous mediaeval churches, hewn out of the living rock at Lalibela deep in the mountain fastness of Lasta had been known in the West since Alvarez saw them when he travelled to Ethiopia with Rodrigo de Lima's Portuguese Embassy in 1520.[3] They were rarely visited subsequently until Prince Ras Mangashia

---

1. Jules Leroy, Stephen Wright and O. A. Jäger, *Ethiopia, Illuminated Manuscripts* (New York, 1961); Jules Leroy, *Ethiopian Painting* (Merton Press, London, 1957).

2. E. Hammerschmidt, *Äthiopische Handschriften vom Tanasee*, I–II (Wiesbaden, 1973–77).

3. Francisco Alvarez, *Verdadera informaçam das terras do Preste Joam* (Lisbon, 1540).

Seyoum built a tiny airstrip in the unbelievably inaccessible mountains in the 1960s. My wife and I visited Lalibela in the early 1970s. We fell hopelessly under the spell of the Ethiopian Highlands which has hit other travellers badly in the past. We sought out Ethiopia experts and met great kindness. David Buxton, Ruth Plant, Beatrice Playne, Ivy Pearce and Edward Ullendorff were all most generous. A group of us suspected that there might be rock-hewn churches in the remote Eastern parts of Tigray, the northernmost province of Ethiopia proper, which had not been described or visited by Westerners before. In the late summer and autumn of 1974 an Oxford University Expedition went to Ethiopia with the objective of finding such churches and among other projects to attempt to survey what rural church libraries contained. Stephen Wright[4] stated: 'the fact has to be recognised that at many places the clergy and monks are firm in their refusal to allow their collections to be seen by any outsiders at all'. We had done some homework. We had met great kindness from Prince Zara Yaqob who was then an undergraduate at Exeter College, and from Lij Yohannes Mengesha who was at St John's College, Cambridge. Yohannes had been very active in facilitating visits to the more inaccessible parts of his home Province. But the outstanding contribution came from the Archbishop of Tigray, Abune Yohannes, and Prince Ras Mangashia Seyoum, the Governor-General of Tigray, who made the expedition possible. Haddis Gebre-Meskel, the Archbishop's nephew, joined the expedition as a quite invaluable member. As he was known to all the clergy, doors opened that otherwise certainly would have remained closed.

Via Addis Abeba we went to Tigray, to Makelle, the Provincial capital, in August 1974. From there we travelled to Atsbi, once an important town on the route of the salt caravans from the Danakil. At Dabr outside the town we set up base camp at over ten thousand feet in the marvellous, hauntingly beautiful highland countryside. From there we explored the country to the edge of the Danakil depression. We found some hitherto undescribed churches during the following six weeks, on one, two or three day expeditions. We covered about a thousand miles on foot during that period. In most churches we were able to compile lists of the manuscripts the churches possessed. We did not always succeed in seeing the books.

4. Stephen Wright, 'Book and Manuscript Collections in Ethiopia', *Journal of Ethiopian Studies*, II (1964), pp. 11–24.

Although an element of suspicion on the part of the priests undoubtedly played a part, the sheer physical difficulties of getting access to the books was often part of the problem. Rarely were more than a few of the MSS kept in the church. Most are preserved in the priest's house which may be miles from the church. In the small square stone-built Tigray house the MSS are kept, often wrapped in Turkey carpets, on the 'first floor' to keep them away from damp, though very occasionally treasures were treated with shocking indifference and marvellous miniatures were at the mercy of rats and mice.

In one instance we had the opportunity of checking the reliability of the priest's list of books against the actual Library. Mikael Debre Selam is only a few hours from Dabr. This fantastic early mediaeval church is carved into the side of an 'amba', a flat mountain, approached by a steep path. On our first visit only a few books were in the church. On our second, we lost our way to the priest's house and got caught by a tropical downpour that turned rivulets into torrents. On our third attempt we were successful. The priests had carried all the books in large bundles in Turkey rugs to the church. All were then collated and photographed and a final tally showed few discrepancies from the titles we had been given on the first occasion.

We compiled lists of the manuscripts in twenty churches. Mikael Debre Selam had forty-four MSS. Some of the other more important churches like Mikael Amba Dera (thirty) and Maryam Dibo (thirty-four) had a wide selection of MSS; most had a dozen or fewer. We had not anticipated finding manuscripts of rare texts, and indeed this turned out to be the case. The titles were the usual service books, the Bible, and Saints' chronicles. Most of the manuscripts were of no great antiquity. All were written on vellum and the standard of workmanship was variable. Alas, there could be no doubt that more recent examples mostly showed declining quality.

After this preamble, something about the book in Ethiopia: Aksum, the ancient capital of the country, was known in Antiquity, for it was described by the author of *Periplus of the Erythraean Sea* in the first century A.D. Splendid stelae and ruins from the early Aksum empire remain to this day. In the fourth century, during the time of King Ezana, Christianity reached Ethiopia. Ethiopic inscriptions, in Ethiopic characters, in South Arabian characters and in Greek in Greek characters have come down to us. Indeed, the Ethiopic inscriptions on tablets and on coins have alone survived. There can be little doubt that manuscripts existed at an early date but none from a very early date have survived. Ge'ez, the ancient Ethiopic language related to Arabic, occupies among the Semitic languages in Ethiopia a position rather like Latin in Europe. Tigrinya is the modern Italian, Amharic modern French. Ge'ez is still used as a church language, but spoken only by a very few churchmen. Unlike Arabic it is written from left to right. It is a phonetic language with a syllabary of consonants with distinguishing variations indicating the value of the vowel following. In 1529 Ahmed Ibn Ibrahim Grañ, a fanatic Muslim, a sixteenth-century Ayatollah, invaded the country and burnt and plundered churches and church possessions, a tragedy comparable only to the Chinese invasion and destruction of Tibetan monasteries in our own time. Very few mediaeval manuscripts survived the holocaust and it is doubtful if more than two pre-thirteenth-century MSS exist, namely the Gospels of the Convent of Abba Garima which have been attributed to the tenth- or eleventh century.[5]

We had not hoped to see any early MSS, but to our surprise, at the remote 'new' church of Maryam Magdalawit, Amba Dera, we found an exceptionally fine dated Gospel book from 1363 with fine borders round Eusebius's Letter and the Canon Tables, and ten very fine full-page miniatures. Plate 1a shows the *Crucifixion*. Note the empty jewelled cross, so characteristic of Ethiopic MSS of this period. Note also the stylised figures of the two thieves and soldiers, and particularly that they all (as in the other miniatures) are shown *en face*. In later MSS malefactors and other undesirable characters are invariably shown in profile. Plate 1b shows the *Fountain of Life*. This decorative theme which probably goes back to the original Canon of Eusebius of Caesarea (*d.* 339) has a close parallel in early Armenian manuscripts of which that from the Second Etchmiadzin Gospels (fig. 1) from *c.* 1000 is a good example, and related examples are found in the Syriac Rabbula Gospels, written in 586 A.D. at the Monastery of St John of Zagba in Mesopotamia. Both the Eusebian Tables and the Enthronement of Christ have similar motifs (see fig. 2), including the birds which in our manuscript are described as 'ostriches', although they clearly are meant to represent peacocks, birds unknown in Ethiopia. It is quite obvious that Ethiopian artists must have had considerable inspiration from Syriac and Armenian sources. Whilst it is generally agreed that most early Ethiopian miniatures are stylised, it is in my view by no means certain that

5. Leroy, op. cit., fig. 7.

that has always been so. The Abba Garima Gospels may be from 1000–1100 A.D. The decorations round the Eusebian Tables (fig. 3) are much less stylised than those seen in fourteenth- and fifteenth-century manuscripts. There is a close parallel in Armenian book illustration, where early illuminations like those in the Mlkhé Gospels of 862 from Vaspuraken,[6] and the Gospels of Queen Mlkhé at San Lazzaro (fig. 4) are naturalistic, but later pictures such as those in the Shukr Khandara Gospels written in the Taurus Mountains[7] are quite stylized.

It has always been assumed that the return to a less stylized form in 'Gondarene' painting was prompted by Portuguese and other Western European influence. It is possible that it was a return, at least in part, to an earlier manner. Leroy, in his splendid monograph, is bothered by the miniature of 'Three anonymous Saints' — beautifully, naturalistically represented young men. The plate is in fact printed inverted in Leroy's book, but when turned (fig. 5) it is obvious that there is a legend, although now hardly decipherable. The middle passage seems to read: 'SIILE: QIDISAT: QOMON:, 'PICTURE OF SAINTS STANDING'. The right-hand legend is only partly readable: 'SIILE: YOTSIN . . ., or FATSIN . . ., or FADIN . . ., 'PICTURE OF YOTSIN . . ., or FATSIN . . ., or FADIN . . .'. The hand appears to be fifteenth-century. Is this not another late survival of an Eastern style? Do we not see in remote Ethiopia, delayed by some hundred years, what happened in Syria and Armenia?

The paintings in the Maryam Magdalawit Gospels are clearly related to those in the Haiq Gospels which was written before 1350, for instance in the treatment of the Crucifixion,[8] where all the malefactors are still shown *en face*. The miniatures have been discussed in some detail in the account of the 1974 Oxford University Expedition.[9] The scribe's use of intercolumnar and marginal tails above and below numerals is very typical of fourteenth-century

6. David Marshall Lang, *Armenia, Cradle of Civilization*, third edition (London, 1980), plate v.

7. *Armenian Art Treasures of Jerusalem*, edited by Bezalel Narkiss (Oxford, 1980), figs. 54, 55, and 56.

8. Jules Leroy, Stephen Wright and O. A. Jäger, op. cit., plate iv.

9. *Rock-Hewn Churches of Eastern Tigray*. An Account of the Oxford University Expedition to Ethiopia, 1974, edited by Bent Juel-Jensen and Geoffrey Rowell (Oxford, 1975), pp. 73–82, plates 97–112, 117, and 118, and coloured frontispiece.

manuscripts. Only one of the Evangelists has achieved a picture, namely St Luke (fig. 6), who is represented seated writing with his reed in the right hand and a tablet or sheet of vellum on a board in his left, with the implements of writing on a table in front of him. The volume was remarkable also for its binding, on one cover decorated with stylised leaves, the other with diagonal lines. The binding is undoubtedly the original — though rebacked, and is unusual for not having the later ubiquitous cross on the side of the cover.

At Mikael Amba, a substantial rock-hewn church, we saw a fragment of seven loose leaves of a fifteenth-century *Senkessar, History of the Saints*, damaged by fire. Three leaves had full-page miniatures in a style characteristic of the fifteenth-century,[10] a further development of the stylised manner, with representations of the Virgin and Child, also found in very similar pictures in the *Gospels* at Gunda Gundie.[11] Related are also the miniatures in the *Gospel Book* (fig. 7) we found at Selassie Gundefru.[12] All are similar to the magnificent series of miniatures in a Ta'amre Maryam — the *Miracles of Mary* from the monastery of Gizen Maryam from the time of King Zara Yaqob (1434–1468), in which gold is used (plate 2). The use of gold-leaf is otherwise practically unknown in Ethiopic MSS. The highly stylised angels are reminiscent of those in the early twelfth-century Spanish Manuscript: *Commentary on the Apocalypse* of Beatus of Liébana from the monastery of Santo Domingo de Silos (British Library Additional MS. 11695).

Ivy Pearce[13] had previously noted how desperately the Mikael Amba MS (of which there was then more preserved) needed care. Leul Ras Mangashia had set up a fairly sophisticated atelier for microfilming and repair of MSS in his home, Emperor Yohannes IV's Palace in Makelle. Our reports, alas, probably were to no avail, for during our stay in Tigray HIH the Emperor Haile Selassie was deposed, and Ras Mangashia had to flee the country with his youngest son. Ironically, as he had done more for his Province and his people than any other man on record. Manuscripts have since disappeared from Makelle.

10. Ibid., plates 92–94.

11. Leroy, op.cit., plates v, vi, and vii.

12. *Rock-Hewn Churches*, plates 95 and 96.

13. Otto A. Jäger and Ivy Pearce, *Antiquities of North Ethiopia*, second edition (Stuttgart, 1974), plate 31.

Second Etchmiadzin Gospels. Western Armenia, c.1000 A.D.
Jerusalem Patriarchate.

2. *Rabbula Gospels*. Mesopotamia, 586 A.D.

a. *Eusebian Tables*.

b. *Christ enthroned*.
Florence, Laurentian Library, Cod. Plut.I,56.

3. *Abba Garima Gospels.* 11th or 12th century.
   Eusebian Tables.

4. *Gospels of Queen Mlkhe.* Armenia, mid-9th century.
   Eusebian Tables (Letter of Eusebius).
   Monastic Library of San Lazarro, Venice.

5. Miniature from 14th century Gojjam MS.

1. *Maryam Magadalawit Gospels.* Tigray, 1363 A.D.

a. *Crucifixion.* Notice the empty, jewelled Cross.

b. *The Fountain of Life.*

2. *Miracles of Mary.* Gizen Monastery. Mid-15th century.
King David paying homage to the Virgin Mary and Christ.

a. *Life of Abba Aregawi Za-Mikael.* 17th century. First Gondarene style. *The Nine Saints.* Note that the fourth Saint from the left carries a manuscript in a bag.

b. *Life and Miracles of St. Giyorgis.* Second quarter of the 18th century. Second Gondarene style.

4. *Miniatures by the "Ground Hornbill Artist".* Mid-17th century.

a. *Gebre Menfes Quedus.*

b. *Crucifixion.*

6. *Maryam Magdalawit Gospels*. Tigray, 1363 A.D.
St. Luke.

7. *Selassie Gundfru Gospels.* Tigray, 15th century.
The Virgin and Child and St. John.

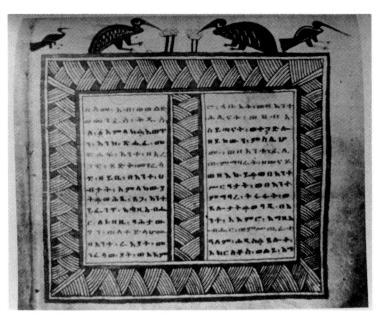

8. *Aregawi Menfasawi.* ? Lalibela, Lasta, 17th century.
Border by "Ground Hornbill Artist".

9. *Book of Enoch (Henok).* Tigray, 1974 A.D.
   Opening page.

10. *Fisalgos (Physiologus.)* Shoa, 1982 A.D.
Opening.

A few of the later manuscripts we saw were adorned with miniatures. The finest was a *Life and Miracles of St Mikael* at Maryam
Wukro Dera profusely illustrated with full-page and small miniatures.[14] These are of good quality, and probably mid-eighteenth
century. In this manuscript the manner of painting has again changed.
It is an example of the so called second Gondarene style, characteristic of the pictures in the vast majority of surviving illuminated
Ethiopic MSS. This manner had briefly, in the seventeenth century,
been preceded by a new school of painting, probably developed at
King Fasilides's Court at Gondar. The best examples of this, the so-
called first Gondarene style, of which plate 3a is one, can be works
of art of great originality. With consummate skill the artist has
produced a splendid composition with relative few means, with strict
economy of colours and design. Perspective is lacking as in most
Ethiopian art. The first Gondarene style was short-lived, and was,
towards the end of the seventeenth century, followed by a much
more realistic, less stylised form of painting, the second Gondarene
style, which as mentioned above, is that found in most manuscripts
with pictures. Although some are very remarkable, as works of art
they compare unfavourably with the miniatures of the first Gondarene period. Interestingly, whilst the book hand in most seventeenth-
century manuscripts is small, in the eighteenth century the letters
tend to become larger, and indeed often very beautiful in the grander
manuscripts, in sharp contrast to the often stereotype, repetitive
designs of the miniatures. Plate 3b is a typical example of a miniature
from a large handsome manuscript of the *Life and Miracles of St
Giyorgis*, Ethiopia's Patron Saint. This book was probably taken by
Emperor Tewodros from one of the churches he robbed in Gondar
for his proposed Library of the projected Medhane Alem Church at
Magdala. It was taken from there by a member of the British Expedi-
tionary Force under Napier in 1868. The tortures to which the hapless
Saint is subjected are shown in gruesome detail in the many miniatures. Note how in the picture reproduced the malefactors are shown
in profile, whereas 'the good' appear *en face*.

In many of the Gondarene paintings the European influence is
obvious. The Portuguese may have brought prints in the sixteenth-
and earlier seventeenth centuries. We know that one artist used the
1591 Arabic Bible cuts by Roberto Tempesta as models for his

14. *Rock-Hewn Churches*, plates 85 and 86.

paintings. British Library MS Oriental 510 is one of a small number of surviving examples of this.

The colophons were sometimes informative, both for help with dating (and this could be very difficult on palaeographic grounds alone), and for information about scribe, donor, and cost. At Mikael Debre Selam, a *Getsew*, a small folio in a good twentieth-century book hand in double columns, bound in stamped goatskin, related that: 'Woisero Desta Yeh Degela gave it for 30 dollars 1949' [Ethiopian Calendar = 1956/7], and it was written by the scribe 'Ques Hagos Reda'. A *Miracles of Mikael* in a good mid-eighteenth-century hand with second Gondarene style miniatures was 'given by Adera Giyorgis . . . during the reign of Yoas'. Yoas reigned 1755–69, so this is a useful guide to a date after which it could not have been written.

A *Kedase*, a folio in eights, written in a fine eighteenth-century hand, was a recent acquisition, for an inscription records that Habte Giyorgis bought it on 21 December 1957 [Ethiopian Calendar = 1964/5] for 90 dollars and gave it to Mikael Debre Selam, whilst a *Kedase* in quarto in a square nineteenth-century hand was given to the same rock-hewn church by Gebre Tsadick who had bought it for sixty dollars.

The Church's *Gospels*, a folio in a good eighteenth-century hand, was bought by Mezgebe Selassie. As often there are in it notes of land transactions, in this instance in Amharic. Mention of Tekle Giyorgis [I, 1779–1784] and Abune Yosab again help narrow down the approximate date. Among the books of *Maryam Dibo*, two give us names from recent Tigray history. A small quarto *Life of Abune Mesih* in a fine early twentieth-century hand says: 'Dej [azmatch] Hailu Dera, his baptismal name Hailemaryam gave this book to Maryam Dibo . . . during the reigns of Menelik the Second and the Archbishop Abune Petros and Abune Matewos. Ras Seyoum, son of Emperor Yohannes and the children of Behole both old and young gave it to Maryam Dibo in 1904 [1911/12]'. A quarto *Dersane Mikael* in a fair mid-twentieth-century hand contains a very informative colophon: 'Praise be to God and St Mikael, for I have finished it well during the Reign of Emperor Haile Selassie and our Bishop Yohannes and our Prince Seife Mikael [the baptismal name of Leul Ras Mangashia Seyoum]. I, Aba Felsa Fesema Tseyon Kekema have sold this book, Dersane Mikael on 12 May 1953 [1960] to Ato Abraha Zewelde and Woisero Lemlem Wakka for 38 dollars'. A quarto *Miracles of Mary*, written in 1956 [1963/4] by Re'ese Debr

Gebre Alfa cost fifty-six dollars, whilst a quarto *Getsew* was sold for one hundred and fourteen 'shillings' [= fifty-seven dollars]. Reference to Abune Yohannes and Ras Mangashia was found in manuscripts in other churches, e.g. in a large quarto *Miracles of Mary*, which interestingly has double dating: 'this book is finished in the 505th year of Mercy in the year of Mercy 1960 [1967/8] during the reign of Atse Haile Selassie and our Prince Seife Mikael. It is finished by the hand of the penniless Habte Selassie. This book belongs to the elder Atse Demaryam who ordered it to be written for her money and gave it to Mikael Amba'. It is difficult to reconcile the two dates, for if the former was the 505th year in the thirteenth Great Lunar Cycle [each of 532 years] since the Creation [B.C. 5492], the date would have been 1921. If on the other hand it represents the 505th year of the third Great Lunar Cycle in the Era of Martyrs (A.D. 284), when the third cycle began in A.D. 1349, it gives us a date 1854 (1861/2) which clearly is impossible. For the very difficult problem of dating Ethiopian MSS the reader is referred to Buxton's discussion.[15] One has a sneaking suspicion that the modern scribe found it as hard to work out the date by the ancient method of dating as we now find it to decipher it. Mention of the reigning monarch and other dignitaries in the colophon as in the example given is a great help.

Maryam Dibo, though a rebuilt church, had an unusually full collection of MSS (thirty-four). One of the most interesting was a small quarto *Aregawi Menfasawi* written in a good seventeenth-century hand in two columns; the opening page has an elaborate geometrical border in black and red surrounding both columns of text, with, at the head of the frame, two smaller birds and two larger feeding stylised birds, resembling ground hornbills (fig. 8). Identical birds are found in the miniature of St Luke in the remarkable quarto *Gospels* in the British Library (Oriental MS 516, Wright XLI) which has a similar border opposite the miniature of St Mark. These decorations and miniatures would appear to be the work of one seventeenth-century artist who quite without influence from the Gondarene School developed his own quite remarkable, highly sophisticated geometrical style. An example of the British Library miniatures has been reproduced in colour by Leroy.[16] In the early seventies I acquired for my own collection four small quarto miniatures by the

15. David Buxton, *The Abyssinians* (London, 1970), pp. 186–88.

16. Leroy, op. cit., plate lv (St Luke).

same artist; plate 4 shows two: *Gebre Menfes Kedus*, a local Ethiopian Saint who according to tradition is clothed in his own hair, and the *Crucifixion* which in its simplicity makes an extraordinary impact. They are reproduced in colour which alone does justice to their subtle pigments. The artist has been discussed in further detail elsewhere.[17]

Although books were printed in Ethiopic type in Europe from the early sixteenth century (Potken's *Ge'ez Psalter* appeared in Rome in 1513) mostly intended for the Roman Catholic (unsuccessful) missionary efforts during that century and the first part of the next, printing only began in Ethiopia at the end of the nineteenth century. Even though large numbers of books have appeared, mainly in Addis Abeba and Asmara, manuscripts continued to be made in the mediaeval manner. It was noted earlier that we did not see rarer texts. To that generalisation there was one exception. I was shown a seventeenth-century MS of *The Book of Enoch*. That apocryphal Old Testament Book has only survived in its entirety in the Ge'ez translation. Like James Bruce who first brought the text to Europe at the end of the eighteenth century, I desired an Enoch. We arranged with Abune Yohannes's scribe, the deacon Amaha Selassie Gebre Kristos from Tembien that he would copy the MS in September 1974 for one hundred and ten Ethiopian dollars. Amaha Selassie went to the market and bought ten goatskins which he took to Menewie Monastery in Tembien, where they were made into vellum. He then wrote the book and bound it in red locally dyed, blind-stamped goatskin over wooden boards. The colophon is dated 25 December 1967 [1 Jan. 1975]. Fig. 9 shows the first page, the hand is quite competent. Fig. 10 shows an opening from an even more recent MS. One of the rarest Ge'ez texts, but one of great interest to a medical man is *Fisalgos*, the *Physiologus*, a collection of information about animals and plants, which was translated into Ge'ez in the Axumite period. It survived in Ethiopia, but was suppressed by the Church in Europe where it once had been popular. Only late Greek MSS have survived, so the early Ge'ez version is of great interest. An Ethiopian friend, a bibliographical scholar, knew where a copy of the text was to be found, and most generously had it copied for me. Albeit written on paper, the hand is of considerable beauty, and an opening of the volume is shown as a final example of a fine 1982 hand.

17. B. E. Juel-Jensen, 'The Ground Hornbill Artist of 17th Century Ethiopic Manuscripts', *The Book Collector*, 26 (1977), pp. 61–74.

The mechanics of preparing the vellum, of the writing and binding of manuscripts, as well as the time allowed for producing standard works are described at some length in Dr Sergew Hable Selassie's *Bookmaking in Ethiopia*.[18] This well-illustrated book is the only work on the subject.

This short survey has not covered, indeed could not hope to cover in depth, the whole history of the development of the Ethiopic manuscript. It is to be hoped that a profusely illustrated monograph one day may appear in which the considerable expertise of, for instance, such great connoisseurs as Jules Leroy and Stanislaw Chojnacki, to mention but two experts, will give us more. Unhappy Ethiopia is still suffering from oppression and internal strife and hunger. Books and manuscripts have been burnt, churches closed and destroyed. Shades of Grañ. We hope that peace will soon return, fear depart, and that scribes again may be able to pursue their peaceful business, and that the barbarians may not succeed in ruining and destroying a fine culture.[19]

The writer is grateful to Mrs Diana Spencer for permission to reproduce a photograph of the miniature from the Gizen *Miracles of Mary* (Plate 2).

18. Sergew Hable Selassie, *Bookmaking in Ethiopia* (Leiden, 1981).

19. Since this lecture was given Stanislaw Chojnacki has published his monumental *Major Themes in Ethiopian Painting. Indigenous developments, the influence of foreign models and their adaptation from the 13th to the 19th century* (Franz Steiner Verlag GBMH, Wiesbaden, 1983). It is essential reading for anyone who wishes to understand Ethiopian art.

HOWARD MILLAR NIXON spent the greater part of his professional life on the staff of the British Museum Library, becoming a Deputy Keeper in 1959 and head of the Rare Book Collections in 1966. He was widely acknowledged as an outstanding authority on the history of bookbindings and his status as a scholar was recognised by numerous distinctions, including appointment as Sandars Reader in Bibliography at Cambridge (1967–68), as Lyell Reader in Bibliography at Oxford (1978–79), and by the award of the Gold Medal of the Bibliographical Society (1978). In 1983 he was appointed OBE. He was Librarian of Westminster Abbey from 1973 until his death in February 1983.

The literature of English bookbinding

HOWARD M. NIXON

Hardly anything of note appeared in print on the subject of English bookbinding before the nineteenth century, when T. F. Dibdin included in his various bibliographical works a certain amount of information — typically inaccurate — on the topic. The first English attempt at a history was the work of John Hannett, writing under the pseudonym of John Andrews Arnett, who published in 1837 *An Inquiry into the Nature and Form of the Books of the Ancients; with a history of the art of bookbinding.* Most of the information that it contains is concerned with continental bookbinding and much of it is now known to be inaccurate. When he did discuss English work, he did not betray any great knowledge of the subject and he achieved the remarkable triumph of never even mentioning the name of Mearne.

In 1881 Joseph Cundall published the first full-length general English history of the subject, *On Bookbindings Ancient and Modern*; this was followed in 1893 by Sarah T. Prideaux's *An Historical Sketch of Bookbinding*, and in 1894 by W. S. Brassington's *History of the Art of Bookbinding* and H. P. Horne's *The Binding of Books.* All of these have some value but include almost everything that was then known on European binding and all suffer considerably from swallowing the assertions of Guglielmo Libri, the Italian book thief of the mid-nineteenth century. They are now highly dangerous reading for those who do not know more recent literature. There was also at this time a useful spate of large colour-plate books, with slight and unhelpful texts but with valuable illustrations. The earliest of these was H. B. Wheatley's *Remarkable Bindings in the British Museum* (1889). In 1891 came the catalogue of the Bookbinding Exhibition of the Burlington Fine Arts Club — full of fakes and mis-attributions, and deceptive colour-plates, but still very useful — and in the same year Brassington's *Historic Bindings in the Bodleian*

Library. In 1893 R. R. Holmes produced his book with colour-plates (some misleading) and the very minimum of text on the bindings in the Royal Library at Windsor — almost all acquired since the accession of William IV, since the earlier royal libraries had gone to the British Museum. W. Y. Fletcher followed this up in 1895 with his *English Bookbindings in the British Museum* and then, with the exception of Edward Almack's *Fine Old Bindings* of 1913, this type of colour-plate book became too expensive to produce.

For the first quarter of this century the history of English gold-tooled bindings was, I regret to say, left almost entirely in the hands of my predecessor at the British Museum, Cyril Davenport, who, to my mind, is the perfect example of the value of a university education. He did not have one. He came into the Museum straight from school, with some artistic ability, and proceeded to set himself up as a writer on almost any artistic subject. His first small book on *Royal English Bookbindings*, published in 1896 and based very largely on the British Museum collections, is not too bad. He followed up with three books published by the Caxton Club of Chicago which are at least delightful to look at. The first, on *Thomas Berthelet* (1901), attributes every pre-1560 English gilt binding to this important English printer. He did on one occasion submit a bill to Henry VIII for bindings, but there is no evidence that he owned a bindery himself. He may have done so, but the bindings attributed to him by Davenport quite clearly come from at least five different shops. A similar book on Samuel Mearne, in 1906, attributed every fine binding of the reign of Charles II to this binder, and Davenport's third book, on Roger Payne, 1929, is only better because it was largely 'ghosted' by C. L. Ricketts, a member of the Publications Committee of the Caxton Club. Davenport must have been nearly eighty years old when it was published. His most notorious book is, however, his *English Heraldic Bookstamps* of 1909. Victor Scholderer, the British Museum's very distinguished incunabulist, told me of how, one day in the North Library at the British Museum, as a junior member of the staff, he was offered a section of the proofs of this book to read. About a week later Scholderer rather apprehensively returned the proofs to Davenport, who grew more and more purple in the face as he noted the growing number of corrections on each page and eventually burst out explosively with 'Good God, boy, if I made all those corrections I wouldn't make any money out of the book at all' and threw the lot into the wastepaper basket. In consequence staff copies of this book in all reputable libraries are corrected from E. Gordon Duff's copy in the Cambridge University Library and they should have further corrections from the Appendix to H. J. B. Clements's 'Armorial Book-stamps and their owners' in *The Library* of September 1939 (pp. 132–35). To take an example – Davenport's identification of the arms of William Covert prove to be 'probably those of Sir Walter Covert' and of the thirteen quarterings Davenport got just two right and eleven wrong. Identification of arms on bookbindings is never easy, since you very seldom get the heraldic colours or tinctures shown. Davenport's method was apparently to look up the arms in Papworth – totally disregarding any form of genealogical investigation – and write down the first name that took his fancy.

Now we can turn to the people who really put together the facts about English bookbinding history and we must start with W. H. James Weale, an interesting character who spent much of his life in the Netherlands. He returned eventually to take charge of the library of the Victoria and Albert Museum and his main work is an obscure little catalogue of the bookbindings there – not then a particularly important collection – and his own important collection of rubbings of bindings from the libraries of the Netherlands and England. Volume 2 – the catalogue of three hundred and twenty-five bindings and nine hundred and fifteen rubbings came out in 1894. Volume 1, the introduction, appeared in 1898 and is remarkable among the bookbinding literature of its period for restricting itself to fact and avoiding speculation. This does not mean that every word in it is now still accepted as true. He knew the Canevari bindings were not bound for Demetrio Canevari, but he followed the prevailing belief that the 'Maioli' bindings were all Italian, and rather surprisingly attributed the bindings for the Belgian sixteenth-century collector to the uncle of the true owner, Marc Lauweryn. But Weale stuck largely to fact, and his two volume catalogue is still a useful, though expensive, work.

In France remarkably little interest has been taken in the country's blind-tooled bindings, but in Germany, the Low Countries and England there has been a marked tendency to begin at the beginning. In England Strickland Gibson's excellent and scholarly *Early Oxford Bindings* appeared in 1903. It is a very useful book still and a model of what such a book should be, with full descriptions of thirty-three blind-tooled Oxford bindings produced before 1640, with plates of the majority; illustrations of ninety-four single tools and twenty-eight rolls used on them; a chronological list of Oxford binders from *c.* 1180 to 1640; extracts from the Bodleian accounts concerning binding; and an excellent introduction. Equally important in its knowledge, attention to ascertainable fact, and fullness is G. J. Gray's *The Earlier Cambridge Stationers and Bookbinders* which like Gibson's book was published by the Bibliographical Society and appeared in the next year, 1904. The other great expert of the history of English binding at this period was E. Gordon Duff. His notes on binders published from his Sandars lectures as *The Printers, Stationers and Bookbinders of Westminster and London from 1476 to 1535* (1906) and *The Provincial Printers . . . and Bookbinders to 1557* (1912) are of considerable importance, but the annotations on his own collection of early blind-tooled bindings included in the catalogue when those bindings were sold at Sotheby's, 16 March 1925, are disappointingly few, although valuable as examples of how to catalogue bindings. The annotations, like anything Duff wrote, are valuable but one could wish that they were more numerous. His most valuable piece on binding history was outside his normal period, 'The Great Mearne Myth', which was published by the Edinburgh Bibliographical Society in 1918. His central thesis, that Mearne never bound a book in his life, has been subsequently proved incorrect, but he provided a great deal of most useful information on other English binders of the period.

Beginning in 1926 we get another explosion of books — this time on gold-tooled bookbindings — but now, unlike the majority of the books of the nineties, the new books were based on sound research and deep knowledge. They were mostly the work of G. D. Hobson, a partner of Sotheby's. But I will mention first E. P. Goldschmidt's *Gothic and Renaissance Bookbindings* of 1928 because, although it deals mainly with European rather than English books, it contains an introduction which is still required reading for anyone taking an interest in the history of binding. Goldschmidt — Dutch by national-ity but educated in Vienna — was a wealthy book collector in pre-first war days at Cambridge where he numbered among his friends Rupert Brooke and Sir Geoffrey Keynes. After the post-World War I crash in Vienna he found himself obliged for the first time to work for his living and turned himself into the most learned of English booksellers. After the publication of his book on bindings Goldschmidt moved on to the study of medieval manuscripts, but Geoffrey Hobson, although exceedingly knowledgeable on almost every artistic subject, remained largely faithful to bookbinding. Of his first two published books which both appeared in 1926, *Maioli, Canevari and others* was almost entirely concerned with French and Italian bindings and *Thirty Bindings* — an account of some unpublished bindings selected from those exhibited by the First Edition Club at Sir Philip Sassoon's house in Park Lane — was two-thirds foreign. But among the English binders who first appeared in this book was Alexander Cleeve; Dr H. M. Davies's signed binding by him was then the only one known; it is now in the Victoria and Albert Museum. Robert Steel also made his first appearance in binding literature in this book with a binding from Hobson's own collection (now in the Walters Art Gallery at Baltimore) which has a signed presentation inscription from the binder.

The following year Geoffrey Hobson gave the Sandars Lectures at Cambridge and these were published in considerably extended form in 1929 as *English Binding before 1500*. In this book, which contains his earliest study of the 'Romanesque' bindings of the twelfth- and thirteenth centuries, he was the first person to suggest that these bindings were not, as even Weale had thought, all English. Further studies on these bindings which he published in *The Library* in 1934– 35 and 1938–39 made it clear that, as the total known rose to over one hundred, the great majority were produced in Paris, and the only certain English examples are three produced in Winchester in the mid-twelfth century, and three London ones, which were probably bound some thirty years later, about 1180. And not only did the French produce the great majority of these Romanesque bindings, but — though Hobson never quite admitted this — I am reasonably certain they produced the earliest ones. They also produced one of the most interesting, a gilt example in the Pierpont Morgan Library, which is probably thirteenth-century.

In the same year, 1929, Geoffrey Hobson also published *Bindings in Cambridge Libraries*, a book with a distinctly troubled history, as he tells us in the Preface. It was begun by two Trinity men, N. F. Barwell and Dr H. M. Davies in the first decade of this century in an attempt to continue the series of colour-plate books of the 1890s. Twenty-five plates had been printed in colour and seven more in monochrome with drawings of binders' tools, when, we are told, 'a series of mishaps made it impossible to proceed'. In 1922 the Cambridge University Press purchased the plates and C. E. Sayle began to prepare it for publication, but he died before he had done

more than assemble some further notes. Hobson in 1925 'reckless of
the sinister history of the book' and little knowing what he was
undertaking, offered to edit the book, and in fact found he had to
rewrite it almost completely. He did a magnificent job, but, hampered
by the already printed plates of binders' tools, got into some difficulties with the English bindings of the Restoration period. The
King's Binder, whom H. M. Davies had invented and for whom he
had produced a plate of tools, was abolished by Hobson himself in
the book I shall mention next. The Queens' Binder has subsequently
been dissected into four. The 'Sombre' Binder has caused some confusion, since almost every English binder of the period did some work
in the sombre style. And the only suggested English shop of Charles
II's reign that has preserved its integrity is that of the Devotional
Binder.

In 1940 Hobson published the nearest thing that exists at present
to a history of English bookbinding, his *English bindings in the
Library of J. R. Abbey*. It contains a wealth of new information on
the subject and throws much new light on many of the binders first
treated in *Bindings in Cambridge Libraries*. Henry Evans makes almost
his first appearance (he had been in Seymour de Ricci's *British signed
bindings in the Mortimer L. Schiff collection*, but without any
worthwhile text) and the work of Roger Bartlett of Oxford was also
identified for the first time. Another newcomer was Richard Balley,
the specialist in backless bindings, and there was much new information at every period from H. Cony, *c.* 1491, to Madeleine Kohn in
1939. Geoffrey Hobson's last important work on English bookbinding
— although there is much valuable material in Sotheby's catalogues
from the early 1920s to his death in 1949 — was his *Blind-stamped
panels in the English Book-trade*, published in 1944, and this leads
us to the next important figure in English bookbinding history,
J. B. Oldham.

Oldham was a passionately devoted member of Shrewsbury School,
first as a boy and then as a housemaster, and when in 1932 a serious
breakdown forced him to give up teaching and running a house, he
was made Librarian. He then turned to the study of blind-tooled
English bindings. After producing *Shrewsbury School Library
Bindings* in 1943, he continued with *English blind-stamped bindings*
in 1952 and *Blind panels of English binders* in 1958, leaving com-
paratively little for other students in the field to glean. His collection
of rubbings is now in the Department of Printed Books at the British

Library. To give an idea of his thoroughness, he recorded one hundred and forty-seven examples of bindings signed by Garrett Godfrey and three hundred and eight by Nicholas Spierinck, both of Cambridge, although he added the note when he had found four hundred and seventy-three with the mark of John Reynes, 'to which many others must doubtless be added'. Curiously enough he always regarded these signatures as those of binders. I do not think there can be any doubt that they in fact appear as the names or initials of booksellers, rather than binders, although probably all these three combined both trades.

I have mentioned that schoolmastering and Shrewsbury School meant much more to Oldham than anything to do with bookbindings. To have been in his house at Shrewsbury was an almost certain claim to his eternal friendship and perhaps the only exception to this rule was Graham Pollard, who may have been the only member of that house to become in early youth a member of the Communist Party. Pollard subsequently proved himself to be Shrewsbury School's most famous bibliographer and his wide-ranging interests came to include the history of bookbinding. Three important articles by him appeared in *The Library*. The first was on 'Changes in the style of bookbinding, 1550–1830' which appeared in 1956; the second in 1962 was on 'The Construction of English twelfth-century bindings'; and the third was 'The Names of some English fifteenth-century binders'; it came out in 1970 and is a very important follow-up of Hobson's and Oldham's work in this field. A fourth article on 'Some Anglo-Saxon book-bindings' appeared in the Spring 1975 number of *The Book Collector*. It was a very happy coincidence that Graham Pollard was President of the Bibliographical Society when Oldham was awarded its Gold Medal. On presenting it all was forgiven and forgotten and Pollard was received back among 'my boys'.

Collectors of bookbindings have sometimes been tempted into writing on the subject and Lt Col W. E. Moss, who sold his books at Sotheby's in 1937, not only wrote three monographs on the subject but printed two of them on his private press. He then gave copies away to a few libraries, collectors, and students of bookbinding history, over a period of several years, making corrections and additions as time went on, so that there are almost as many states of each book as there are copies. He had a genius for genealogical research and worked out the successive owners of books in which he was interested with astonishing skill. But he was also rather prone to allow 'flair' rather than research to guide him in other matters and his books have to be approached with caution. The first was *Bindings from the Library of Robt. Dudley, Earl of Leicester, K.G.*, privately printed at the Manor House Press, Sonning-on-Thames, 1934, my copy of which has an Appendix, dated May 1944. This book contains a valuable list of seventy bindings, an untrustworthy attribution of the books to different binders, and an ingenious but manifestly incorrect attempt to solve the mystery of the code signature which appears in many of the books. *The English Grolier: a catalogue of books from the library of Thomas Wotton*, followed in 1941. Once again there is a splendid and well-researched list of well over one hundred bindings, but the text is based on an implausible guess that all the elaborate bindings were produced in Canterbury. They are in fact all French. The latest classification of these Wotton bindings is that of Mrs Mirjam Foot in the first volume of her Henry Davis binding catalogue. Colonel Moss also produced in typewritten form an account of some of the elaborate bindings executed for Matthew Parker. I have a photocopy of this, sent me by W. A. Jackson of Harvard. Moss assumed that all these books had been bound at Lambeth for Parker, but they seem to come from four different binderies.

Most of the books discussed so far have concentrated on the bindings and what could be learned about them. Ellic Howe took the opposite approach and concentrated on the binders. His *A List of London Bookbinders, 1648–1815*, published by the Bibliographical Society in 1950, is one of those books which got written almost by accident, growing out of preliminary work for his *The London Bookbinders, 1780–1806*. It records what can be discovered about bookbinders in the records of the Stationers' Company and although this is slight in comparison with the material available for Paris binders – or for those of Oxford and Cambridge – it nevertheless does give us a working basis on which to build. Unfortunately before 1648 the Company's records do not normally reveal the actual branch or branches of the book trade practised by its members; and after 1815 all the fine binders in the capital had moved from the City of London to Westminster, and were no longer members of the Stationers' Company. From about 1780 much of the best work done in England was by binders from Germany, who found that the average English gentleman could afford more elaborate bindings for his library than could the average German prince. In addition, the German binders were much better educated and from a much higher social class than their English counterparts. In the period 1780–1820 Roger Payne and Edwards of Halifax stood almost alone against Baumgarten, Kalthoeber, Walther, Staggemeier and Welcher and many another German binder. Even Charles Lewis, the leader of the London trade in the 1820s and 1830s was the son of an immigrant German binder, Johann Ludwig, who like many of the others came from Hanover. For the binders of this period the two dictionaries of Charles Ramsden are valuable reference works – *Bookbinders of the United Kingdom (outside London), 1780–1840*, and *London Bookbinders, 1780–1840*, published in 1954 and 1956 respectively.

I am restricting myself to books and articles about English bookbinding, but am including general books on binding which contain a considerable amount of material on English work. The presence of Dorothy Miner's great Baltimore Exhibition Binding Catalogue of 1957 is well justified on this ground; it was an astonishingly fine show and I shall always be grateful to Dorothy Miner for giving me the opportunity of seeing all the books before the show opened and of helping with the final stages of the cataloguing.

Eschewing false modesty I am now going to say something of some of my own writings about English bindings. My first article on a bookbinding appeared as 'English Bookbindings No. 1' in Volume 1, No. 1, of *The Book Collector* in the Spring of 1952. A reviewer in the *Times Literary Supplement* remarked that 'at this rate it will take 25 years for Mr Nixon to reach his century'. However I persevered, only broke the series once, when I wrote about an Irish binding, and – *The Book Collector* coming out quarterly – duly completed my century in twenty-five years and three months. The articles were revised and published as *Five Centuries of English Bookbinding* in 1978. My first book was written for the Roxburghe Club in the days when that club only printed one hundred copies. *Twelve books in fine bindings from the library of J. W. Hely-Hutchinson* (1953) is therefore almost unfindable. In addition to describing the bindings illustrated, it has essays on English royal library bindings, on English binding in the second half of the seventeenth century, and on the German binders in England. There are two further pieces on French binding, one on Wotton bindings, and the other on those made for Grolier.

My next solid publication is equally difficult to find: *Broxbourne Library, Styles and designs of bookbindings from the twelfth to the twentieth century* (1956) is a description of 119 of the most valuable books in the library of Albert Ehrman, which was subsequently presented to the Bodleian by his son. The English articles of the greatest interest in this book are, perhaps, first that dealing with the Cambridge binders of the seventeenth century, in which I followed up an important article by J. C. T. Oates in the *Transactions of the Cambridge Bibliographical Society* (1953), entitled 'Cambridge Books of Congratulatory Verses, 1603–1640, and their Binders'. My conclusion was that in the first half of the century some were by Daniel Boyse and some by Henry Moody. And secondly the article on the Restoration period and which bindings I considered could be safely attributed to Samuel Mearne. This has a triumphant appendix announcing that I had discovered that Mearne had been apprenticed to a bookbinder, and that he had therefore himself certainly bound books before launching out into higher things in the book trade.

My next publication in book form is equally difficult to obtain, not because it is now so expensive, but because it *was* so cheap. It is entitled *Royal English Bookbindings in the British Museum* and was published on the occasion of the Queen's visit to the Museum in 1957. Published originally at three shillings it was remaindered – rather unnecessarily the author thought – at two shillings or one and six. It has now of course disappeared completely.

It has always been my intention to produce a reasonably solid history of English bookbinding, and I am hoping that my Lyell Lectures at Oxford in 1979 will eventually be in a fit state to publish. Meanwhile I have written one or two chapters and salted them well away in Festschriften. 'Early English gold-tooled bindings' in the great four-volume Festschrift for Tammaro de Marinis, printed by Giovanni Mardersteig (*Studi di bibliografia e di storia in onore di Tammaro de Marinis*, 1964) goes up to 1558. The next chapter, 'Elizabethan gold-tooled bindings' appears in *Essays in honour of Victor Scholderer* published in Mainz in 1970.

In 1974, as my final fling at the British Museum – by then the British Library – I put on an exhibition *English Restoration Bindings: Samuel Mearne and his contemporaries*, the catalogue of which was largely based on my unpublished Sandars lectures at Cambridge. It included all the surviving Samuel Mearne bindings for the Royal Chapels, and the work of other binders of the period, such as Fletcher, the Royal Heads Binder, the four Queens' Binders, the Naval Binder and others.

My final egotistical act will be to draw your attention to another piece lost in a Festschrift, an essay on 'Harleian bindings' which I contributed to *Studies in the Book Trade in honour of Graham Pollard* (1975). Page 99 of Joseph Cundall's 1881 *On Bookbindings, Ancient and Modern* says of the Harleian Library 'The binders were Elliott and Chapman, who attained to some eminence in their day', and a careful reading of his paragraph about them suggests that he knew they were two distinct firms. But the indexer to that book treated them as a firm called Elliott & Chapman, and so they remained until 1943 when, in his Shrewsbury School book, Oldham showed that if you looked at Humfrey Wanley's diary, which has been in the Department of MSS at Bloomsbury since the eighteenth century, it was absolutely clear that Elliott and Chapman were rival binders. Seeing the diary only in manuscript and for a limited time, Oldham came to the conclusion that Elliott did all the best work and unfortunately attributed the Harleian binding in the Shrewsbury School Library to him. Now that Dr and Mrs Wright have published the diary, and I have been able to consult the Elliott bills deposited at the British Library by the Duke of Portland, it has become possible to sort the binders' tools quite clearly. Elliott and Chapman did an almost equal amount of the best work for Harley, but the Shrewsbury book turns out to be by Chapman.

Lest I leave the impression that I am the only person in England who has written on the history of bookbinding in the last thirty years, I must hasten to disabuse you. Although most of A. R. A. Hobson's published work has been concerned with foreign rather than English bookbindings, he maintained for a quarter of a century at Sotheby's the high standards of cataloguing them which had been set by his father, G. D. Hobson. Bryan Maggs, himself a bookbinder, has also shown wide knowledge and a scholarly approach in the catalogues of bookbindings recently issued by Maggs Bros.

A. R. A. Hobson's article written in conjunction with A. N. L. Munby, on Major J. R. Abbey's great collection of bindings in *The Book Collector*, Volume 10 (1961), is also relevant here. Munby's wide knowledge of the history of the English book trade extended also to the binders of books, and he published a number of valuable articles in periodicals. In *The Book Collector*, in addition to the article just mentioned, he contributed 'Collecting English Signed Bindings' to Volume 2 (1953) and 'Notes on Thomas Gosden' to Volume 24 (1975). For the *Transactions of the Cambridge Bibliographical Society*, he wrote three pieces in the first volume, 1949–53; they deal with: 'Notes on the Binding of Ushaw College XVIII c.9b', 'Chirm's Banded Bindings', and 'Windham and Gauffecourt'. Also from Cambridge, as already mentioned, comes J. C. T. Oates's article in 1953. There have been some developments since then in views on these bindings, most recently summed up by Mrs Foot in Volume I of her Henry Davis Catalogue.

The seed that Strickland Gibson sowed in Oxford certainly fell on good ground and yielded fruit that sprang up. In the last thirty years six members of the Bodleian staff have written about bookbindings. I. G. Philip first published in 1951 a picture book, *Gold-tooled Bookbindings* and, under his Keepership, Giles Barber, David Rogers, and Paul Morgan produced the excellent catalogue of an exhibition, *Fine Bindings, 1500–1700, from Oxford Libraries*, which was held at the Bodleian in 1968. Philip also wrote an article, 'Roger Bartlett, Bookbinder', in Volume 10 of *The Library* (1955) in which he produced important new material on the work of that binder, later supplying me with further evidence that enabled me, in the same journal in 1962, to allay his fears that Bartlett had not bound some of the books attributed to him. W. O. Hassall, Librarian at Holkham, as well as being on the Bodleian staff, has written on Hatton's bindings in 'The Books of Sir Christopher Hatton at Holkham' in the June 1950 number of *The Library* and first brought to light the binder Jean Robiquet whose work he illustrated in 'Portrait of a Bibliophile II: Thomas Coke, Earl of Leicester', in *The Book Collector*, Autumn 1959. Giles Barber, while he was on the Bodleian staff, contributed to *The Library* in 1962 'Notes on Some English Centre- and Corner-piece Bindings, c.1600' and in 1964 'Richard Dymott, Bookbinder'; essays by him in the *Bodleian Library Record* include in 1970 'The Vice-Chancellor's Official New Testament', and in collaboration with David Rogers 'A "Duodo" Pastiche Binding by Charles Lewis' in 1969. David Rogers wrote in *The Book Collector* for 1975 on 'An Unpublished Early Oxford Binding', which covers a Boccaccio manuscript c.1480. R. J. Roberts completes the Bodleian sextet with a bibliographical note in the June 1957 number of *The Library* on 'Sir Christopher Hatton's Bookstamps'.

This valuable flow of writings by members of the Bodleian staff leads us on to T. W. Hanson, father of one of Bodley's Keepers of Printed Books, and himself the expert on the Edwards family, late eighteenth-century booksellers and bookbinders of Halifax, who established themselves in London and patented a method of decorating vellum bindings with paintings on the underside of portions of the vellum rendered transparent. Hanson first wrote about the family and the bindings in the *Bookbinding Trades Journal* in 1911, discussed them further in a long contribution in the *Transactions of the Halifax Antiquarian Society* in 1912 and added some more information in *Book Handbook* in 1948.

As the late evening recreation of a busy Headmaster of Eton, Sir Robert Birley wrote a series of articles on the history of the College Library, all containing new information on bindings and their makers. 'The history of Eton College Library', which appeared in *The Library* in 1956, introduced a new and splendid example of the close connection between bookbinding and insobriety in the person of a binder named Williamson of whom Sir Dudley Carlton remarked 'he hath commonly his hands full of work, and his head full of drinck'. This was followed in the same journal in 1960 by his study of 'Roger and Thomas Payne: with some Account of their Earlier Bindings'. To *The Book Collector* of 1956 Sir Robert contributed an article on 'The Storer Collection in Eton College Library' which introduced us to a collector of bindings in the same class as his contemporaries C. M. Cracherode, whose books are at the British Library, and H. G. Quinn, benefactor of Trinity College, Dublin. 'The Library of John Reynolds at Eton College', a more recent article in *The Book Collector*, Spring 1975, discussed the English blind-stamped bindings in that library. In the same number of *The Book Collector*, which was devoted to the history of bookbinding, A. I. Doyle wrote an important piece on 'Hugh Hutchinson, Bookbinder of Durham', who had hitherto appeared in the literature of the craft as an exceedingly vague figure. Another contributor to this number was William S. Mitchell, the authority on Scottish bookbinding, on this occasion discussing 'A New 16th-century Panel Stamp', with portrayals of the Virgin and Child and the Image of Pity side by side, which is very likely to be English and is unknown elsewhere. Mitchell also contributed to *The Library* in 1960 an article on 'A Signed Binding by James Fleming, Newcastle, *c.*1740'. The 1962 volume of *The Library* contained Neil Ker's 'The Virgin and Child Binder, LVL, and William Horman' in which he discussed another unpublished panel stamp. His *Early Pastedowns in Oxford Bindings* has much to interest the student of bindings. In the Autumn 1977 *Book Collector* John P. Chalmers contributed an article on 'Thomas Sedgley, Oxford Binder', which produced a considerable amount of new information on binding in that city in the first half of the eighteenth century. In particular he was able to identify the series of unusual polychrome Oxford bindings of the 1720s and 1730s as Thomas Sedgley's work, and it seems very probable that Thomas was the son of Richard Sedgley, whose death was recorded by Thomas Hearne in 1719. The Summer 1981 number of the same journal contains the most extensive piece yet written on the work of the Comte de Caumont, 'A French Bookbinder in London' by Claude Boisset-Astier, which lists fifty bindings by him. The majority of these are now at Cambridge in the Fitzwilliam Museum. Number 13 of the list, formerly in the Holford and J. R. Abbey collections, was presented by Mr K. H. Oldaker with the rest of his collection of bindings to the Westminster Abbey Library earlier this year. A catalogue of this gift is now in the press.

On twentieth-century English bookbinding there is a fairly extensive literature including M. Wieder Elkind's article in the Autumn 1975 *Book Collector* on 'Jewelled Bindings 1900–39', most of which were the work of Sangorski & Sutcliffe. Dorothy Harrop has contributed to the same periodical between 1972 and 1981 an impressive series of 'Craft Binders at Work', dealing in turn with William F. Matthews, Anthony Gardner, Roger Powell, S. M. Cockerell, H. J. D. Yardley, Ivor Robinson, Jeff Clements, B. C. Middleton, C. P. Smith, Elizabeth Greenhill and Sally Lou Smith. Books on their own bindings have also been produced by Edgar Mansfield and Philip Smith.

Paul Needham's *Twelve Centuries of Bookbindings, 400–1600* (1979) includes valuable discussions on ten or a dozen important bindings for English owners, varying from the eleventh-century Judith of Flanders to Queen Elizabeth I, which are now the worthy possessions of the Pierpont Morgan Library, New York. John Harthan's *Victoria & Albert Museum Bookbindings* is a valuable introduction to the holdings of that institution which have been greatly improved since the 1930s. Mirjam Foot's Catalogue of the splendid Henry Davis Gift to the British Library will eventually comprise three volumes. Volume I appeared in 1978 containing discussions of the work of, and much new information on, the King Edward and Queen Mary Binder, E. D., the MacDurnan Gospels Binder, John Bateman, the Squirrel Binder, Daniel Boyse, Thomas Dawson, Ed Moore, Christopher Norris, and Roger Payne, as well as important binders from other European countries. Volume 2, likely to appear before the end of this year, will include full descriptions and illustrations of every English and some of the foreign bindings – a unique achievement for the catalogue of a library of this size.

Turning from the decorative to the structural side of bookbinding, Graham Pollard's articles on techniques have been mentioned above, but the standard work on the subject is *A History of English Craft Bookbinding Technique* by Bernard Middleton, first published in 1963. The author is himself an outstandingly successful craftsman, with a good historical background, and, when repairing early books, has made the most of his opportunities to study their construction. He has also edited in the 1962 volume of *The Library* a fascinating broadside in the Pepys Library called 'The Bookbinder's Case Unfolded' which gives a splendidly detailed account of all the processes involved in binding, clearly intended as a justification for a rise in prices.

So far our view has been almost entirely restricted to bookbinding by hand in leather, vellum, or parchment. I do not intend to venture deeply into the development of machinery for bookbinding, but the early development of binders' cloth is relevant. The first important contribution on binding and casing in cloth was Michael Sadleir's *The Evolution of Publishers' Binding Styles* which appeared in 1930. John Carter followed in 1932 with *Binding Variants in English Publishing, 1820–1900*, and by 1935, when he issued *Publisher's Cloth . . . 1820–1900*, it was fairly well established that at some date not long before 1825 a primitive calico was being used for binding some of William Pickering's *Diamond Classics* with Archibald Leighton as the main binder responsible for its development. Douglas Leighton's Dent Memorial Lecture, *Modern Bookbinding: a survey and a prospect*, came out in 1935, and deals largely with the first introduction of machinery into the process of binding, or more correctly casing, books, while in *The Library* of June 1948, in an article, 'Canvas and Bookcloth', he drew attention to the use of an earlier style of binding fabric, the canvas used on schoolbooks and the like from at least as early as 1770 until after the introduction of binder's cloth.

A still earlier stage was covered by David Foxon in his 'Stitched Books' in the Spring 1975 *Book Collector*. This deals with books from the late sixteenth century to the close of the eighteenth which, instead of being properly sewn, were 'stabbed' or pierced from front to rear through the inner margin. Lionel Darley's *Bookbinding then and now* (1959) is a useful summary of nineteenth-century progress and Ruari McLean's *Victorian Publishers' Bookbindings* (1974) gives a valuable account of the decorated cloth work of this period.

Finally the most precious of all English bindings must be mentioned, the Stonyhurst Gospels, quite probably buried with St

45

Cuthbert in the year 698, at present on loan from Stonyhurst College to the British Library. There is an extensive literature on this precious book, the most recent and authoritative being the technical description of the binding by Roger Powell and Peter Waters in T. J. Brown's *The Stonyhurst Gospel of Saint John,* published by the Roxburghe Club in 1969.

The most recent bibliography of books and articles on English bookbinding is to be found at the end of my *Five Centuries of English Bookbinding* (1978). It includes a few articles not mentioned above.

BERNHARD FABIAN is Head of the English Department of the Westfälische Wilhelms-Universität, Münster. He specialises in seventeenth- and eighteenth-century English literature, and is currently editing the catalogue of early English books in Göttingen University library. He is also working on a bibliography of German translations of the works of British authors between 1680 and 1810.

The first English bookshop on the Continent

BERNHARD FABIAN

1

Though the literary relations between England and the Continent have been studied for more than a century, there is as yet no account of the Continental demand for English books as it developed through the centuries. Nineteenth-century book historians have explored isolated episodes in the traffic of books. Thus we know, if only in rudimentary outline, of the sale of books of English origin at the Frankfurt Book Fairs in the seventeenth century. These books were intended for the scholarly reader of the period, and nearly all of them were written in Latin. They were elements in a large European network of communication for which the Latin language was the proper medium of exchange.[1]

The situation changed in the eighteenth century with the discovery of England by various European nations. There was a French discovery of England (which can be followed in Voltaire's *Lettres philosophiques* and many other sources), and there was also a German discovery of England, which had momentous consequences for the cultural and literary life of the country. In the second half of the century English culture rose to a position of European pre-eminence, and the English language emerged as a major European language – ultimately to become the lingua franca of the modern world.

Though in the eighteenth century, hundreds, if not thousands, travelled to England in search of information about the country, its inhabitants and its institutions, the medium for the assimilation of English thought and literature on the Continent was primarily, and in most cases exclusively, the printed page. Regardless of what England

---

1. For specific references see my survey, 'English Books and their Eighteenth-Century German Readers', in *The Widening Circle: Essays on the Circulation of Literature in Eighteenth-Century Europe*, edited by Paul J. Korshin (Philadelphia, 1976), pp. 117–96.

ultimately meant, the source of knowledge was a book or a journal in the original language or in one of the many translations that were speedily produced. Thus, the eighteenth-century expansion of English culture must, to a large extent, be regarded as a bibliographical phenomenon. The bibliographical aspect is one of its fundamental aspects and it may well prove *the* fundamental aspect.

We have recently developed a new awareness of the need to apply the principles of enumerative bibliography to almost everything printed in a given period. We have also developed an awareness of the need for studying the channels of distribution through which printed material reached the reader. If we apply this to the study of the eighteenth-century impact of English culture on the Continent, two tasks present themselves to the bibliographer: the compilation of as complete a bibliography as he can produce of the translations and reprints of English texts on the Continent; and the reconstruction of the ways and means through which texts of English origin reached the Continental reader.

The little story which I want to tell of the first English bookshop on the Continent is one of the preliminary results of an attempt to identify the mechanisms both national and international that were at work in a process of assimilation that has few parallels in the relations between two national cultures.

2

On 8 August 1787 the *Staats–und Gelehrte Zeitung des Hamburg-ischen unpartheyischen Correspondenten* carried, among various other advertisements, the following announcement:

> The Reputation of our English Authors being well known and established, and their writings dear and difficult to procure in this Country, I propose establishing an English circulating Library; with a View of furnishing those Ladies and Gentlemen in and about Hamburgh who are their Admirers, with a cheap and easy Opportunity of perusing them.
>
> In Case a sufficient Number of Subscribers soon appear to indemnify my Risk and Trouble, this Library shall be opened on the 2d. of January 1788, and commence with at least 2000 Volumes of well chosen Books in every Branch of polite Literature, both instructive and amusing for the Gentleman and the Scholar; to which all the best new Publications shall be added

as they appear, with several of the monthly Magazines and other periodical papers and Pamphlets; the Catalogue of which shall be timely ready for Delivery, and due Notice given.

As its Existence depends merely on a competent Number of Subscribers, it is hoped those Ladies and Gentlemen who wish to see a Thing of the Kind, will send in their Names and Addresses as speedily as possible; and not delay till they see whether it succed or not, as in many Cases it often happens; for that would be subverting their own Wishes.

Annual Subscribers to pay 24 Mk. Lubish, and half yearly 14 Mk. for which they will be allowed three Volumes at a time, as often as they please. Those who live at a considerable Distance may have more, on paying proportionably.

The Subscriptions to be paid on the opening of the Library; and none taken for less than six Months.

Books will likewise be had for Sale, at very little more than the London Prices; but no Credit given.

The announcement was signed by a William Remnant, who gave 'Auf dem Gänsemarkt' as his address. His name must have been known at least to some readers of the paper. He was a Londoner and had come to Hamburg several years before. In 1785 the Hamburg marriage register noted that Remnant had been a resident in Hamburg for six years.[2] Remnant was born in 1749 or 1750 and he must have come to Hamburg at the age of twenty-nine, where he married Margaretha Catharina Richters. His occupation was given as 'Sprachmeister' (language teacher). Remnant would seem to have continued being a teacher of English until he became a bookseller in 1788.

Remnant made his first public appearance on the title-page of a book called *Merchants Letters, Translated from the German of J. C. Sinapius; His second edition. By William Remnant, Teacher of the English Language in Hambro'*. The translation of this book of model business letters was published in 1783 by J. G. Virchaux, one of the smaller Hamburg booksellers; the firm ceased to exist when Virchaux went to Paris two years later.[3] With his letter book Remnant wanted to break into a market that had previously been dominated by Johann

2. Fol. 548; Wednesday, 27 July 1785.

3. See Hermann Colshorn, 'Hamburgs Buchhandel im 18. Jahrhundert: III. Die kleineren Firmen', *Aus dem Antiquariat*, 30 (1974), A 81 (*Börsenblatt*, Frankfurter Ausgabe, 29 March 1974).

Karl May's *Commercial-Letters according to Professor Gellert's Rvles: Translated from the Last German Edition: By Capt. J. G. Smith, Esq. B.A.,* published in Bremen in 1768. Characteristically Remnant recommended his book by drawing attention to the modern and idiomatic style of his letters. By contrast, May's book was, in Remnant's words, 'replete with circumlocutions, tautologies and ambiguities'.

Remnant's idea of a lending library was in line with his activities as a teacher. Apparently he wanted to make another (and, possibly, for himself more profitable) contribution to the spread of modern English literature by supplying reading matter to those who knew English or were about to learn English as a new and increasingly indispensable foreign language.

Whether or not Remnant's idea was inspired by English lending libraries, the task of importing from England some two thousand volumes must have appeared a daunting task. We do not know what happened in the months that followed the announcement. At any rate, Remnant seems to have reconsidered his plans. Maybe he received an insufficient number of subscriptions; maybe he came to the conclusion that his project was premature; maybe he received indications that his prospective customers preferred to buy books rather than to borrow them. As a result, he decided to open a different sort of business.

On 1 January 1788 a new announcement appeared. This time it was conspicuously placed in *The British Mercury*, a paper written in English and edited by Johann Wilhelm von Archenholz, the most successful journalistic intermediary between England and Germany at a time when German interest in England was particularly strong. (From the King's health to new plays at Drury Lane, Archenholz reported practically everything with astonishing speed.) Under the heading, 'English Library, established at Hamburgh' Archenholz inserted the following note:

> The Public are hereby acquainted, that a valuable Library of new, old, and many very scarce English Books, in all Arts and Sciences, is now opened by WILLIAM REMNANT, at his House in the Gaense-Markt, Hamburgh; where Gentlemen may be sure of being supplied with any Quantity, for ready Money, at a cheaper Rate than they can procure them themselves from England.
>
> Orders for any Quantity of English Books not in his Cata-

logue, and also for Maps, Globes, mathematical, astronomical, chirurgical and other Instruments, Music, Copper-Plates Ec. punctually and expeditiously executed; and sent to any Distance, on previous Security being given for the Payment on Delivery at the Post.

Good Allowance to Booksellers; and all Letters postpaid, duly answered.

Catalogues, Price 6 Pence, may be had at the Place of Sale.

In other words, Remnant had opened a combination of modern and antiquarian bookshop. Perhaps this was better suited to the requirements of the situation in Hamburg than a lending library would have been. Still, Remnant appears to have been uncertain about the future of his new business. Maps, globes, and scientific instruments were also offered for sale — obviously in the expectation that they would attract a different kind of customer. The market for these was fairly safe. Engravings and maps were in demand as attributes of a new chic Anglophile style of life. And precision instruments, both surgical and scientific, were indispensable products of the superior technology of England.

In view of the many difficulties that beset the book trade with England, Remnant apparently thought that large-scale imports of books were both possible and desirable. Whether he planned to act as an agent for provincial booksellers only or whether he envisaged some sort of collaboration with the leading Leipzig booksellers is difficult to determine. As early as the 1750s some Leipzig firms, notably Johann Wendler, had tried their luck as wholesalers, but the precise nature of their business relations with English publishers remains to be established.[4]

Finally, Remnant had not completely given up the idea of establishing a lending library, though it no longer dominated his plans. On 25 January 1788 the supplement to the *Kaiserlich privilegirte Hamburgische Neue Zeitung* contained a notice of the new bookshop, and this suggests that books could not only be bought but also be borrowed from Remnant. If a lending library existed, it must have been much smaller than originally planned.

4. See 'Die Messkataloge und der Import englischer Bücher nach Deutschland im achtzehnten Jahrhundert', in *Buchhandel und Literatur: Festschrift für Herbert Göpfert*, edited by Reinhard Wittmann and Berthold Hack (Wiesbaden, 1982), pp. 154–68.

The 'English Library', as it came to be called, appears to have grown rapidly, and two months later it was obvious that it was more than a modest success. On 17 March 1788 Archenholz informed the readers of *The British Mercury:*

> Mr. REMNANT, an Englishman settled at Hamburgh, has given Notice to the Public by various Advertisements of the establishment of an English Library, where Books of all sorts, ancient and modern, published in the British Empire, maps. prints Ec. are to be got, or easily procured. It will be pleasing to the Lovers of English Literature to hear, that this usefull Undertaking, the only one on the whole Continent, that is, or ever was to be found, is prospering beyond all expectation. The Orders for English Books pour on Mr. R. from all parts of Germany, and he is promoting this zeal of the Public by making reasonable prizes. Considering the difficulties by which new English Books were formerly procured, Mr. R. deserves the highest encouragement.

It would seem, then, that Remnant with his bookshop not only filled a 'niche' in the market but that he performed a real and valuable service. That Archenholz did not tell lies to his readers is borne out by an unpublished letter, which he addressed to the well-known Leipzig publisher Göschen with the intention of establishing a business relationship between Remnant and Göschen. 'The rush of customers', Archenholz writes, 'is unbelievable . . . Piles of letters arrive every day'.[5]

There are indications that in the early 1770s an English-reading public had emerged in Germany. Its size is difficult to estimate but it was sufficiently large for publishers to discern a possible market for reprints of English books. Remnant's success would indicate that this public had rapidly grown. And many of his customers must have been highly pleased at the prospect of obtaining English books at moderate prices. The prevailing situation before Remnant is illustrated by a remark in the *Altonaische Gelehrte Mercurius* in 1772: 'The high price of English books makes them rare in Germany, and thousands who would prefer to read the original texts must resort to translations.'

In March 1789 Remnant himself summarised his early experiences in a note 'To the Public', this time written in German. With a charac-

5. 22 January 1788.

teristic undertone of satisfaction and self-confidence, he thanked his customers for 'the generous support I have received from all sides'. The issue between him and other booksellers was the speed and the reliability of the service. After eighteen months he felt so sure of his performance as a Bookseller that he publicly challenged others to supply English books faster than he could. Wind and weather permitting, he promised to deliver any book not in stock within five or six weeks, rare books excepted.[6]

The most interesting aspect of Remnant's account is his claim that his business had been 'expanding from week to week, beyond the provinces of Germany and Switzerland, to Denmark, Sweden, and Russia'. He also claimed that he exported 'a considerable number of Latin, Greek and other learned works to England and Scotland'. If this is correct (and there is little reason to doubt this statement) Remnant must have been a bookseller of some consequence. With customers in Southern Germany and Switzerland, his bookshop cannot but be regarded as an important centre for the distribution of English books in the German-speaking area. At the same time, his connections with Scandinavia, Russia and, presumably, the Baltic region (with such cultural centres as Mitau) indicate some of the intricate channels through which English authors reached the more remote parts of Europe. Finally, if and when the history of the export of German books to England comes to be written (it began in the late eighteenth century and gave rise to the strong early nineteenth-century English interest in Germany), Remnant will deserve a footnote, if not a chapter, in that account.

3

For some years Remnant's business activities can be followed in some detail. In the first place, Remnant established a close collaboration with Archenholz. Both men profited from it. For Remnant the *British Mercury*, which addressed itself to an Anglophile readership, was the best advertising medium he could wish for. Archenholz, in turn, could not but welcome Remnant's attempt to market English books in Germany: Remnant's customers were prospective subscribers of *The British Mercury*. Thus, Archenholz's motives in reporting on Remnant's 'useful undertaking' were not wholly altruistic.

6. Note in No. IX of his catalogues sent out with *The British Mercury* (see below).

In July 1788 Archenholz went one step further. He informed his readers that

> Mr. REMNANT, English Bookseller in Hamburgh, in order to render himself still more useful to the public, and in gratitude for their generous support hitherto, will, at the end of this month, publish gratis,
>
> No. 1.
>
> of a Monthly Catalogue, of all the new Books printed in Great Britain; with their sizes and prices.
>
> This Article will therefore be left out in the Mercury for the future, as needless; and Mr. Remnant's monthly Catalogue, carefully delivered to the subscribers, in its stead.

Henceforth Archenholz omitted the short lists of new books which he had published from time to time. From August 1788 onwards subscribers of *The British Mercury* received, at fairly regular intervals, monthly catalogues of the books which Remnant offered for sale. Thanks to this arrangement, Remnant's catalogues are preserved, albeit in very few copies. A search through various sets of *The British Mercury* has produced a complete run of the twenty-four catalogues which Remnant issued between 1788 and 1790.

The first catalogue begins with an address 'To the Friends of British Literature'. It is of particular interest as an indication that, despite a number of efforts that had been made to provide information on current English books, access to such bibliographical sources as then existed was apparently difficult. 'The labors of the English press, having been, till now, only known in a very imperfect and divided manner, and at very great expense', Remnant promised his customers catalogues of 'all the new books, new editions and translations, published in the British Dominions' and offered them as 'a welcome tribute of thanks to the public, for their hitherto generous support of the publisher's new undertaking'.

Remnant reminded his customers that the first catalogue was at least in part a retrospective catalogue. Still, the majority of the items offered for sale were new publications. But though new, they were not invariably important. Many were ephemera and cannot even be traced in the British Museum Catalogue. What Remnant listed was a cross-section of what issued from the British press, and his titles do not all give the impression of having been taken from reliable sources. The standard of cataloguing, though not high, is hardly below the level of most contemporary booksellers' catalogues. Some of the information would seem to have been deliberately omitted.

For the first months Remnant handed out catalogues which lack any obvious system of arrangement. Most of them contain between sixty and eighty items, and they are highly miscellaneous in character. Interestingly, in none of the catalogues do belletristic items at first find a place. Beginning with catalogue No. IX, a subdivision into seven sections was introduced. The first section comprises 'Medicine, Arts, History etc.', the second 'Theology', the third 'Politics and Miscellaneous', the next three are composed of 'Poetry', 'Plays', and 'Novels', while the seventh is headed 'New Magazines'. With slight modifications Remnant retained this grouping for the rest of the series.

Remnant's classification is certainly not noteworthy from a bibliographical point of view, but it is of considerable interest to the student of the reception of English literature on the Continent. From the standard accounts of the cultural relations between England and various Continental countries, including Germany, it would appear that the reception of English authors was, first and foremost, a literary phenomenon in the strict sense of the word. Remnant's catalogues provide a different picture. Their arrangment and their contents suggest that the Continental interest in English books was by no means confined to belletristic works. On the contrary, the *belles lettres* were at best one among several fields of interest, and they cannot be said to have been of dominant interest. In many cases medical and scientific books appear to have taken the precedent over belletristic and even humanistic works.

The last decades of the eighteenth century were not one of the most brilliant periods in the history of English literature. They were a period of transition between Neoclassicism and Romanticism, imitative in some respects, pseudo-original in others. Many productions of the period, far from being first-rate, can hardly be called second-rate. Still, they were exported, and Remnant's catalogues provide an index to the kind of literature that was avidly consumed abroad. They offer a glimpse of what the Continental Anglophile, the 'mere' reader of English books, accepted and apparently appreciated.

Remnant's ninth catalogue, the first of the classified catalogues, lists among the new poetical works of the month *Miserio's Vision; or, Four pleasant Epistles to four unpleasant Characters* and *Sick Laureate; or, Parnassus in Confusion*. Goldsmith's *Deserted Village* (eleventh edition) is the only well-known item among more than twenty-five, and Erasmus Darwin's *Botanic Garden* and 'Peter Pindar's' *Poetical Address to a Falling Minister* are the two that can claim a place among the minor poetry of the period. The new novels present a similar picture. The *Vicar of Wakefield*, which was highly thought of in Germany, is listed side by side with *Mammuth; or, Human Nature displayed on a Grand Scale; by the Man in the Moon* and *Zelia in the Desert; or, Female Crusoe*. In all, a selection of titles that is of sociological rather than literary interest.

In selecting his titles Remnant does not seem to have relied on the leading journals such as the *Critical Review* or the *Monthly Review*, which were widely used by readers and reviewers in Germany. His sources appear to have been other journals and possibly daily and weekly papers. The fact that he offered periodicals for sale suggests that his sources were many and varied.

When *The British Mercury* was discontinued in 1790, Remnant stopped publishing his monthly catalogues. Henceforth he appears to have issued annual catalogues. At least one of them, that for 1791, is preserved in one or two copies.[7] It is subtitled 'A collection of new English books, best editions. With an appendix of some second-hand, scarce, and valuable articles'. It consists of sixty-four printed pages and, unless larger catalogues come to light, must be regarded as the most comprehensive eighteenth-century catalogue offering English books to the German reader. It is divided into six sections: 'Dictionaries; Arts, History &c.; Novels and Romances; Pamphlets; and Plays', followed by an appendix comprising antiquarian books. The dictionaries range from *Abercrombie's Gardener's Dictionary* to Young's *Latin and English Dictionary* and include four different editions of Johnson. From the next section one could select 'Adams's practical essays on agriculture' as well as 'Bell's edition of the poets', 'Hepplewhite's cabinet maker's guide' as well as 'Rowley on female nervous diseases'. The novels, listed alphabetically by title, range from 'Adventures of King Richard Coeur de Lion' to 'Zoriada; or village annals'. Plays were offered at five, ten, and fifteen Groschen, with *Cato* in the cheapest and *The Beggar's Opera* in the dearest category. Among the antiquarian authors there were editions of Boyle, Mandeville, Fielding and others, some marked 'scarce' or 'very scarce'. In sum, then, in 1790 a vast range of English books was

---

7. One is now in the Landesbibliothek Oldenburg. It contains a note by Remnant for one of his customers.

obtainable from Hamburg, provided the German customer could afford them.

4

Remnant's bookshop existed for nearly a quarter of a century. Though his business activities cannot be traced in every detail, one can catch an occasional glimpse of what went on. Thus, as early as 1790 Remnant planned to be at the Leipzig Fair 'with a large Collection of the best and most modern english Books'.[8] He appears to have prepared a special catalogue for this occasion, but no copy of it can be traced. At any rate, among the specialities he planned to bring to the Fair were ancient authors in contemporary or near-contemporary English editions. As his monthly catalogues reveal, at least some of them must have been Foulis and Baskerville editions. The German demand for English editions of the Classics was considerable throughout the eighteenth century. How many of them were indeed brought to Germany is illustrated by Wilhelm Brüggemann's *View of the English Editions, Translations and Illustrations of the Ancient Greek and Latin Authors*.[9] It is the most extensive eighteenth-century bibliography in this field and was compiled by a German from German library resources.

Another important development of the late 'eighties and early 'nineties is also reflected in Remnant's catalogues: the spread of English printing in Germany. About the time Remnant opened his shop the most successful of the various reprint publishers in the German-speaking area set to work: Johann Jakob Thurneysen in Basle.[10] Though Thurneysen's reprints can be found in many libraries, the information on him as a printer of English books is scanty. He had English advisers, who selected titles for him and saw the books through the press, so that everything he produced is of a high technical standard.

As early as January 1788 Archenholz informed the reader of *The British Mercury* that 'Mr. Thurneisen . . . has . . . undertaken to print

8. Announcements appeared in his catalogues.

9. Stettin, 1797; Supplement 1801. Reprinted New York (n.d.).

10. See Martin Germann, *Johann Jakob Thurneysen der Jüngere, 1754–1803: Verleger, Buchdrucker und Buchhändler in Basel* (Basel, 1973), and my survey, 'The Beginnings of English-Language Publishing in Germany in the Eighteenth Century', in *Books and Society in History*, edited by Kenneth E. Carpenter (New York, 1983), pp. 115–43.

the best classical Books published in the English language, upon the subjects of Philosophy, History, Poetry, &c. in order to favour the increasing passion for English Literature, shewn in all the most civilized countries'. Several months later Remnant inserted a note in one of his catalogues: 'all the English Works published by Mr. Tourneisen . . . are to be had of Mr. Remnant; at the usual Prices'. The first reprint produced by Thurneysen was an edition of Gibbon's *Decline and Fall of the Roman Empire,* which was then in the process of publication. In view of the distribution of English literature on the Continent it is interesting to note that the prices which Remnant charged for Thurneysen's reprints were between a third and a quarter of the prices of the original English editions. The lower prices were due to two factors: labour was cheaper on the Continent than in England; and all reprints were in octavo, regardless of the format of the original editions.

Thurneysen also reprinted works of current interest. A particularly instructive example is George Keate's *Account of the Pelew Islands.* The book came out in July 1788, and was so much in demand that Remnant could not procure enough copies. In October the second edition was out and his customers were informed that 'for the accommodation of those Gentlemen who could not get any of the 1st Edit. R. had got over many Copies of this 2d Edit'. Thurneysen obtained a copy of the first edition (in quarto) and produced an octavo edition (for which the map had to be re-engraved and the index adjusted) with such speed that within less than a year the book was again available in Hamburg and could be included, roughly a quarter of the London price, in Remnant's monthly catalogue of books 'published in the English Dominions'.[11] All this suggests that the student of the reception of English literature on the Continent must take into account more than one system for the distribution of English works. (Thurneysen, incidentally, built up a wide network for the sale of his reprints. He had an agent in Gotha, who acted as his representative at the Leipzig Fairs, one in Strasbourg, and one in Paris.)

In the early nineties Remnant made an attempt to expand his business. While English interest in German books was growing stronger every year, there were only very few German booksellers in London: Griffith in Paternoster Row, Giesweiler in Parliament Street, Escher in Gerrard Street, and Bohn in Frith Street. Among them, one James Remnant made a sudden appearance. He seems to

11. See his catalogues for October 1788 and June 1789.

have opened his shop in St John's Lane, West Smithfield, and moved later to High Holborn and to High Street, St Giles. In 1795, if not earlier, James Remnant issued a *Catalogue of Ancient and Modern Books (Particularly German),* and another catalogue appeared in 1800, which informed the customer that 'every Article of Literature published in Germany, Denmark, Switzerland, and Russia, [will be] speedily procured to any amount for prompt payment on delivery'.[12]

The Remnants were a family of businessmen. One of them was a timber-merchant. Another opened a book bindery in 1785, which continued for almost a century. James Remnant was a brother of William. As a German traveller to England disclosed at the beginning of the nineteenth century, it was William who set up a business for James, but James was not nearly as good a bookseller as his brother. After about a decade the export-import scheme collapsed and James Remnant went out of business in about 1804.[13]

One of the remaining traces of his venture is the *Universal European Dictionary of Merchandise* in twelve languages, which Philip Andreas Nemnich brought out first in German in 1797 and two years later in English. It was a joint publication by three booksellers: William Remnant, James Remnant, and Joseph Johnson, the well-known late eighteenth-century London bookseller and publisher. That Johnson did business with the Remnants can perhaps be taken as an indication of their good standing. If so, the credit must go to William Remnant.

Surprisingly, Remnant did not try his luck as a publisher on a larger scale. He did some small things such as engravings of Hamburg and its local costumes but apparently with no great success. He may also have been associated with two books by L. T. Rede, *A Sketch of Hamburg* (1801) and *An Essay on the Laws of England* (1802). At any rate, he did not publish reprints of English authors. One can only guess at the reasons.

Remnant moved several times within Hamburg, first from the Gänsemarkt to the still more central Dammthorstrasse, where he did business during the 1790s. Several of his visitors and customers left

12. A copy is in the British Library.

13. See Philip Andreas Nemnich, *Neueste Reise durch England, Schottland und Irland, hauptsächlich in Bezug auf Produkte, Fabriken und Handlung* (Tübingen, 1807) and his earlier *Beschreibung einer im Sommer 1799 von Hamburg nach und durch England geschehenen Reise* (Tübingen, 1800). Each contains notes on the London book trade.

short accounts of the bookshop. One is Karl August Böttiger, who edited the then widely read *Journal des Luxus und der Moden*. He came from Goethe's Weimar and was struck by the air of intellectual cosmopolitanism which pervaded Fauche's French bookshop and Remnant's English bookshop. Most of the numerous English and American publications, he mused, would hardly ever reach Weimar, and the few that arrived would be delayed for months.[14]

Three years later a little company of English travellers visited the shop. They had just arrived in Hamburg and found it 'an ugly City that stinks in every corner'. One or two days later they went to Remnant's shop. One of them wanted to cash a money order with Remnant. He had received it from Joseph Johnson – 'without any poems sold to him; but purely out of affection conceived for me, & as part of any thing I might do for him'. The three travellers returned repeatedly, and one of them jotted down: 'The Shop near the Jung-fernstieg – delightful young men in it – fine heads of Jacobi, Wieland, Schiller, & Goethe'. Another entry in the diary runs: 'Sate an hour at Remnant's. Bought Percy's ancient poetry, 14 marks'. Remnant's shop, then must have been a pleasant place, nicely decorated and attractive to browsers. Unfortunately, the little company left Hamburg about two weeks later without further reporting on Remnant. It consisted of Samuel Taylor Coleridge and William and Dorothy Wordsworth.[15]

Towards the end of his career Remnant opened the kind of circulating library which he had originally planned. It would seem that he was more or less forced to do so. In June 1802 another Englishman, Thomas Harbridge (about whom nothing is known) announced his plan of establishing a lending library in Hamburg.[16] Apparently as a countermove, Remnant inserted the following advertisement in the local papers:

At the repeated Request of many Friends to English Literature,

14. *Literarische Zustände und Zeitgenossen,* edited by K. W. Böttiger (Leipzig, 1838), II, pp. 64–65.

15. Coleridge, *Collected Letters,* edited by Earl Leslie Griggs (Oxford, 1956), I, p. 417, and *Notebooks,* edited by Kathleen Coburn (London, 1957), I, No. 340; *Journals of Dorothy Wordsworth,* edited by Ernest de Selincourt (Oxford, 1967), I, p. 31.

16. *Privilegirte wöchentliche gemeinnützige Nachrichten von und für Hamburg,* 19 June 1802.

on the 2d of January next will be opened, a very valuable and extensive

English Circulating Library,

which shall vie with the best similar Institution in London; including all the interesting newest English Books, Pamphlets, Journals &c, as soon as they can be procured. Plans and Catalogues may be had Gratis of the Proprietor William Remnant, English Bookseller, No. 52., next Door to the golden A.B.C., near the Exchange, Hamburgh.[17]

Copies of the plan and catalogue have not yet come to light, so that we cannot form an idea of the nature and the size of the project. The only safe assumption seems to be that by the beginning of the nineteenth century the demand for English reading matter had grown in Hamburg.

Very little information is available for the years that followed the addition of a lending library to the bookshop. In 1810 his address was Hohe Bleichen — still in the very centre of Hamburg. One would like to know whether this can be taken as an indication of prosperity or must be regarded as a symptom of decline.

From the beginning, it will be remembered, Remnant offered globes and scientific instruments in addition to books. A year or two later he also sold such elegant paraphernalia of the English style as would be appreciated by his Anglophile customers. There were, for instance, 'Ladies Pocket books . . . bound in red Morocco, with plates, a pencil and silver cap' and 'Ditto ditto in red sheep' as well as 'Gentlemens ditto in red Morocco'. The novice was informed that 'these annual pocket books contain several useful articles of instruction, information and entertainment for both sexes; besides a number of ruled pages for memorandums &c'.[18] It is in this context that a note in the Hamburg directory of 1803 puzzles the reader: 'Handelt auch mit engl. Patent-Medizin' — 'also sells English miracle medicine'. It is impossible to say what this implies. We do not yet know enough about the role which English and Scottish medicine and quackery played in eighteenth-century Germany.

The directory of 1810 has a still more puzzling note: Remnant also sold 'health chocolate and medicine'. In the same year 1810, on 1 July, Remnant died at the age of sixty. His widow continued the business.

---

17. Ibid., 8 December 1802.

18. Catalogue for October 1789.

Apparently she moved again, for in 1811 her address is given as Admiralitätsstrasse. And the information attached to the address reads: 'Health chocolate, Medicine, Opodeldoc'. No reference to the English Library, no reference to books. One wonders whether books were taken for granted or whether the bookshop had been turned into a health-food shop.

Perhaps we shall never know. On 14 December 1814 August Friedrich Uhlenhoff, an inn-keeper, reported to the police that his mother-in-law, Catharina Margaretha Remnant, had died at the age of fifty-four.[19] An episode in the history of Anglo-German cultural relations had come to its natural end. How important it was remains to be seen. We shall have to identify Remnant's customers. Those that are already known would seem to justify the attempt I have made to reconstruct the story of the first English bookshop on the Continent.[20]

19. *Register des Civil Standes der Stadt Hamburg: 1814: Sterbefälle, No. 8609* (Staatsarchiv, Hamburg).

20. An earlier German version of this paper appeared in *Festschrift für Rainer Gruenter* (Heidelberg, 1978), pp. 122–47. I am indebted to the Volkswagen-Stiftung for the award of an *Akademie-Stipendium*, which enabled me to do further research on the subject.

JOHN HORDEN is Professor Emeritus of Bibliographical Studies in the University of Stirling. He is currently editing *The Dictionary of Scottish Biography*.

A Dictionary of Scottish Biography

JOHN HORDEN

Charles Darwin's *On the Origin of Species* first appeared in 1859. But Patrick Matthew is believed to have anticipated Darwin's theory of evolution by natural selection by almost thirty years. Matthew was a horticulturalist who passed his life in obscurity. Kirkpatrick Macmillan invented the bicycle as we know it. He thus gave transport to millions (and it was recently pointed out in *The Sunday Times* that the brightly-coloured bicycle is replacing the mule as a conveyance in the Middle East). But Macmillan was a simple blacksmith. Quite unlike either of them was a little-known scholar, Professor Hugh Cleghorn, who annexed Ceylon to Britain bloodlessly and by extraordinary diplomatic methods. A Victorian engineer called Robert Davidson was a mechanical genius who invented a printing machine, a lathe, an electro-magnetic locomotive, and other devices. He had no recognition in his own time and is forgotten now. Again to look overseas, there is Mary Slessor, once a mill-girl, but later the epitome of the dedicated female missionary. Her self-taught medical skills and unorthodox methods — such as her practice of fearlessly reproving blood-thirsty and gun-crazed tribal chiefs with a hearty slapping — made her a legend in her own lifetime. What have these five in common? They were undoubted achievers, none of them is noticed in the *Dictionary of National Biography,* and they were all Scots.

That selection of names is, perhaps, a slightly quixotic one. But it could readily be enlarged many times over, and a comprehensive statement would include celebrated names. Indeed the Scots, as a nation, are not well represented in the *Dictionary of National Biography.* It is reasonable to ask why.

To do so is not to suggest that the *Dictionary of National Biography* is less than a majestic piece of work, or that its high reputation is undeserved. But it has limitations that must be recognised. *The Dictionary of National Biography* was conceived in 1882, and contrary to what might be expected of so large a scholarly project it was compiled and published with quite astonishing speed. Sixty-three volumes, containing thirty thousand entries, appeared between 1885 and 1900. Subsequently the work has been continued in a series of volumes each covering a ten-year span. The seven volumes dealing with the years 1901–1970 contain a further six thousand entries. It is difficult to calculate closely how many of the thirty-six thousand lives represented are those of Scots. But a partial count suggests that there are no more than two thousand. That figure is astonishingly low.

Sir Sidney Lee, one of the original editors of the *Dictionary of National Biography,* claimed that it included the names of 'all men and women of British or Irish race who have achieved any reasonable measure of distinction in any walk of life', and he did not exclude malefactors. But, in fact, it is a highly selective work, especially with regard to those notable figures who flourished during the last two centuries or so. As far as they are concerned, limitations of space have effectively required that only about one per cent of all truly eminent Britons are represented. The term 'truly eminent' has, in practice, usually meant that they had been accorded an obituary notice in *The Times* or the *Gentleman's Magazine.* And that, after all, is neither an automatic distinction nor the only indication of achievement. It has also to be remembered that toward the end of the last century Scotland was still thought to be – in quite the nicest way – a trifle peripheral (some Sassenachs apparently believing that Scotland was discovered in 1822 by King George IV and only made respectable by Queen Victoria some twenty-five years later). Thus, from a list of, say, one hundred ornithologists distinguished enough to warrant consideration for an entry in the *Dictionary of National Biography,* the editor would have had room only for one. If the choice eventually lay between a Scot from Edinburgh and an Englishman from London the latter would probably be selected. All told, and without there being any genuine bias against them, the Scots have had rather short measure from the *Dictionary of National Biography.*

The Scots are a very remarkable people (and this is probably the appropriate moment to remark that I am not a Scot). When economic disaster at home, such as Highland clearances or the Industrial Revolution, or what appears to be an innate Scottish determination to excel, has driven Scots overseas they have flourished. The names of emigrant Scots alone provide a chapter of colonial history. As a

correspondent of *Blackwood's Magazine* put it in 1884, 'when colon-
ization came into vogue [the Scot] was foremost among colonists . . .
invariably fortune attended his steps. He opened up new channels of
trade; he wrestled with savage nature, and tamed her into a sub-
missive servant; whenever money was to be made, the proverbial
Scotsman had not long to be looked for'. Indeed, it was recently
estimated that the descendants of Glaswegians alone living outside
Scotland now number ten million.

Even when they have gone to what must, initially, have seemed
strongly alien lands, Scots have adapted in a quite remarkable way.
Consider, for example, the Greig family. Samuel Greig was born at
Inverkeithing, Fife, in 1735. At the age of twenty-eight he was a
Master's Mate in the Royal Navy. He then joined the Russian Navy
and within six years was a Captain. In the war with Turkey, while
commanding a division of the Russian Navy in 1770, he played a
major part in the destruction of the Turkish fleet in the Bay of
Chesme. By the time peace came Greig was a Vice-Admiral, and he
was then given the opportunity of improving the Russian Navy. He
was responsible for numerous innovations. One of these was the
introduction of many Scottish officers. Greig was to die at sea in
1788 on active service under the Russian flag. But by that time he
had been appointed Grand Admiral and had received several orders
of knighthood. Grand Admiral Sir Samuel Greig was in fact the
'father' of the modern Russian Navy.

Both the son and the grandson of Sir Samuel Greig were to be
distinguished in the Russian services. His son, Admiral Alexis Samuel-
ovitch Greig (1775–1845), similarly joined the Navy and fought
bravely in the Russo-Turkish wars of 1807 and 1828–29. Like his
father he was involved in naval reorganisation. He created the Russian
Black Sea fleet. (The Grand Admiral, the 'father' of the Russian navy;
his son, the 'father' of the Black Sea fleet; and looking in a westerly
direction one finds that John Paul Jones from Galloway was the
'father' of the US navy; how many other navies have Scots begotten?)
The grandson of Sir Samuel, General Samuel Alejearitch Greig
(1827–1877), won renown in the Crimean War, especially at the
seige of Sebastopol. Furthermore, as a small demonstration that a
man of Scottish blood, even two removes from Scottish birth, can do
anything, it should be noticed that the General was at one time
President of the Imperial Russian Horticultural Union and made a
notable study of Central Asian flowers. One of these, a tulip, is

named after him. (Whether Admiral Alexis Greig and General Samuel Greig are eligible to be considered as Scottish is a matter to which I will return.)

The Greig family was by no means unique among Scots on account of its connection with Russia. The post of Imperial Court Physician, for example, was held by more than one Scot. Dr John Rogerson, a native of Dumfries, became Court Physician to Catherine the Great. The last Scot to hold that office was Dr Alexander Crichton. He was Physician in Ordinary to Tsar Alexander I in 1804, and after his return to England he was knighted by George IV.

The families of some emigrant Scots have adapted to the point where they have virtually been absorbed. That of John Law of Lauriston (1671–1729) is a splendid example. He came of a well-known Scottish family. But after killing one 'Beau' Wilson in a duel in 1694 he was sentenced to death, and only managed to avoid execution by escaping to the Continent. He established the Banque Générale in 1716, the first bank of any kind in France. He is generally held to have advanced French industry and commerce. His only son, William, who fled to France with him, became a Colonel in an Austrian regiment, and died at Maastricht in 1734. The Colonel's son, James (1768–1828), was created Comte de Lauriston and served as aide-de-camp to Napoleon. He died a Marshal of France.

One more example and the point is perhaps made. George Keith, tenth Earl Marischal, and his younger brother James, were forced to leave Scotland after the 'fifteen'. Both served in the Spanish army. Later George was to be Prussian ambassador in Paris and afterwards in Spain. Eventually he became Governor of Neufchâtel, he was the friend of Rousseau and Voltaire, and he enjoyed the personal regard of Frederick the Great. His brother James was a Major-General in the Russian army and Governor of the Ukraine, and in due course a Field-Marshal in the Prussian army and Governor of Berlin. Versatility must be second nature to the Scot.

From an obscure horticulturalist to a Grand Admiral in the Russian navy; from a Dumfries blacksmith to a Field-Marshal in the Prussian army who was also the brother of a Scottish earl; and from an eccentric professor to a French financier; the number of their like is legion. And then there are the Scots of renown – Scots such as James IV, Mary Queen of Scots, James Boswell, Robert Burns, Thomas Babington Macaulay, Sir Harry Lauder, Earl Haigh, Lady Churchill, Kenneth Clark, and many thousands more. The Scots are indeed a ubiquitous and successful people. Their whole history endorses the validity of a comment made in 1775 by an Englishman, Edward Topham: 'you will find that if any dangerous and difficult enterprise has been undertaken, any uncommon proofs given of patience or activity, any new countries visited and improved, that a Scotchman has borne some share of the performance'. And perhaps most striking of all is the fact that the Scot, no matter how far removed from Scotland, seems never to lose a profound sense of national identity. I think that the moment has come for the creation of a *Dictionary of Scottish Biography*.

The Scottish achievement has inspired many important biographical works: *A Biographical Dictionary of Eminent Scotsmen* (4 vols) which Robert Chambers edited in 1855 is a remarkable example of its kind, although its title was to be echoed innumerable times by compilations like Joseph Irving's *The Book of Eminent Scotsmen* (1881). Specialist biographical works are also readily to be found: F. Michel's *Les Écossais en France* (2 vols, 1862); W. J. Rattray's *The Scot in British North America* (4 vols, 1880); A. F. Steuart's *The Scots in Poland* (1913); and G. Berg's *Scots in Sweden* (1962) are characteristic. Useful though all such works may individually be, they do not aim at comprehensiveness, and their intention is usually that of concentrating only on the great, the eminent, and the remarkable. This is insufficient. What is urgently needed is a single, unified, and, above all, comprehensive *Dictionary of Scottish Biography*. It would include fresh accounts of all the glittering figures that have already been extensively noticed in historical studies and in the specialist biographical dictionaries, of course. But it should also give full recognition at last to the many talented Scots who have never received proper acknowledgement of their achievements. It would be appropriate to national pride and it would unquestionably be an immensely useful reference work. So what form should a *Dictionary of Scottish Biography* take, and how might it be compiled?

First of all I think that entries should be in concise, almost severely factual, form, and should not be of the long interpretative essay type. The reason for that is twofold. I believe that for reference purposes most scholars like to be presented with the facts which they may assess for themselves, rather than to have to disentangle them from the opinions of others. Of course it is historically valuable that the *Dictionary of National Biography* records Sir Leslie Stephen's assessment in 1900 of Sir Walter Scott's reputation (set out in an entry that is twenty-five times longer than the average). But it is more generally useful to have the facts stated simply and clearly. In any case, the interpretative essay needs to be re-written every twenty to fifty years as new material becomes available or as climates of opinion change. Secondly, as far as it is possible to estimate such things in advance I suspect that a comprehensive *Dictionary of Scottish Biography* (hereafter *DSB*) could need to contain at least thirty thousand entries. It would be a massive operation to commission and edit that number of essay-type entries if, as would at present be the case, only strictly limited funds were available.

The type of entry I envisage would be after this fashion:

> HENRY, Robert (1718–1790). Historian. Born 18 February 1718 in the parish of St Ninians, Stirlingshire; son of a farmer. Studied at Edinburgh; licensed as a preacher, 1748; DD Edinburgh, 1771. Presbyterian Minister successively at Carlisle, Berwick, and (first) at New Greyfriars, and (later) Old Greyfriars in Edinburgh. Appointed Moderator of the General Assembly of the Church of Scotland, 1774. His only considerable work was his *History of England* (5 vols, 1771–1785, 6th vol. 1793) for which he received a pension in 1781. Henry's *History* owed its popularity to his having treated the subject under seven subject headings instead of chronologically. The work was the object of unprecedented critical attacks by Gilbert Stuart (q.v.). These failed to damage the great success of the *History* at the time, but Henry's work has now passed virtually into oblivion.

To those essentials I would recommend the addition of two features that are slightly unusual in this kind of biographical writing. First of all I should like to see a brief reference to where a likeness of the subject may be found. If it may conveniently be done this seems to me most desirable. For the most part it need be no more elaborate than a reference by number or by page to a catalogue of one of the great portrait collections such as those of the National Portrait Gallery or of the Scottish National Portrait Gallery. Where, as would frequently occur when a great figure is concerned, there are many portraits, then some choice and recommendation might be made, in such terms as, for example, 'best portrait by Raeburn; still belongs to family (not available to public); copy in Napier College, Edinburgh'. If, as would again happen frequently, the only portrait were an engraved frontispiece in a book, then a reference to one of the standard bibliographies, like the *Short-Title Catalogue* or Wing, would suffice. It might not be possible to discover the portrait of a Dumfries blacksmith, or even of a laird, if reclusive, but I would expect that probably more than half of those to be noticed would have left a likeness. I think that the effort of seeking these would be worth making, and that the resulting reference would add a dimension to the entry.

In a similar fashion I would wish to add a brief reference that would readily identify the coats of arms of those entitled to bear them. There would be no need to describe the full Achievement of Arms. Scottish heraldic law is different from English, and I understand that armorial reference may be made with admirable conciseness.

It will have been noticed that the sample entry just offered gave no indication of the sources of the information. The extent to which an entry in a *DSB* should include a record of its sources would be a perplexing problem. If, on one hand, every statement were to be fully documented, then it would mean that entry after entry would necessarily have the same reference works or standard histories listed among its sources. The most reasonable and practicable solution seems to me at this point to be found in various preliminary lists and blanket statements. These could be keyed, by author or short-title, and the statement made that unless otherwise indicated all information of certain kinds was from these sources. Where, of course, information was derived from a unique source — a letter or an inscription in a book, for example — then that source should be recorded. To get the right balance would not be easy. My own strong inclination in any other context would be to document every statement as fully as possible. But here I should be anxious to avoid overloading any entry, and especially a short one, with a large paragraph of sources. Furthermore, were I the editor of a *DSB*, I should hope that at least fifty years or a century would pass before any revision (as distinct from enlargement) were needed, and I should not want to have extensive reference made to biographies, for instance, that might well be superseded within ten years of publication. It is a very special problem and one which an editor could only solve by keeping it well in mind and modifying his view as the work progressed.

To make sure that a *DSB* attained its maximum usefulness I would add, contrary to normal practice with biographical dictionaries, certain indexes. The dictionary itself would have the entries arranged in alphabetical order of surname (or its equivalent) but this could happily be supported in an Appendix by an index of achievement and by another of place of birth (or association).

The index of achievement would need a number of main headings each with appropriate sub-divisions. Main headings could be 'The Arts', 'Politics', 'Medicine', and the like; under 'Medicine' there would presumably be a distinction made between, among others, 'Physicians' and 'Surgeons', and under the latter, provision for noting various kinds: 'micro-', 'ophthalmic', 'plastic', 'neuro-', and whatever else reasonable taxonomy required. There are several existing, and well-tried, indexes that could provide suitable models.

An index recording place of birth or association would present different, but far from large, problems. For instance, anyone consulting a *DSB* to confirm some fact about Jane Welsh Carlyle (wife of the writer, Thomas Carlyle) might, on noticing that she was born at Haddington, in East Lothian, recall that it was also the birthplace of John Knox, and wonder whether Haddington could claim any other celebrities. Reference to 'Haddington' in a gazeteer-like index should quickly settle the matter. With large towns having many well-known sons and daughters it would be necessary, no doubt, to sub-divide the list of names, ordering it according to the various fields of achievement. Questions to which the index should then have answers would be of the order of 'Have any famous painters come from Dundee?', or 'What Scottish statesmen were born in Aberdeen?', and 'Is Auchtermuchtie the birthplace of any golfer who played for Scotland?'. The place of birth of no small number of distinguished men and women has not been established (or has been concealed). Even if the information were not yielded by research I would expect that it would be possible to name a place of association that would meet the usual purpose of an enquirer. I should emphasise that the lists envisaged would all be based upon, and would have cross-reference to, the information of the main entries of the *DSB*.

Very probably in the course of the work other indexes or lists would propose themselves. An index of pseudonyms might be necessary. The identities 'Lewis Grassic Gibbon' (James Leslie Mitchell) and 'Hugh MacDiarmid' (Christopher Murray Grieve) are still very generally known, but might they not become partially obscured when those writers are as far distant in time as are now 'Isaac Bickerstaff' and 'Gawain Douglas' (both Allan Ramsay)? Perhaps an index of those who habitually used the Gaelic form of their name would also be required. And since the Scots, as a nation, appear to give rather more than common acceptance to nicknames, it might be courteous to provide an index of sobriquets ranging from

'Bluidy Mackenzie' (Sir George Mackenzie of Rosehaugh) and 'Bobbing John' (John Erskine, eleventh Earl of Mar) to the 'Wizard of Yester' (Sir Hugo de Gifford) and the 'Wolf of Badenoch' (Alexander Stewart). But what of 'Betty Burke'? In which index should go the name assumed by Bonnie Prince Charlie when escaping after Culloden disguised as Flora MacDonald's maidservant? But in addition to indexes, simple lists might have a part to play. Lists of Scottish holders of certain high offices or sporting titles could provide a service: Prime Ministers, Cabinet Ministers, Archbishops of Canterbury, Open Golf Champions, and so on.

To begin with, some boundaries of the work would have to remain imperfectly defined, since various possible limitations could only become clear as progress were made. But to recognise that state of affairs is not to suggest that any planning should be postponed. Indeed, quite the contrary is to be urgently recommended.

Many of the typographical conventions and methods of presentation required in a reference work of this kind would need to wait upon the agreement of designer and printer. But the prudent editor should have formed his opinions long before: too much bold type makes a page look either as if it has been hit by a line of bullets or as though it has measles; over-indulgence in abbreviations (though saving space) may cause a scholarly paragraph to read like an estate agent's advertisement; exuberance with italic type or parsimony in leading can make an entry difficult to read; there is ample opportunity for spoiling a good work through indifferent design. The only safe course for the editor would be to have considered in advance, and as a deliberate exercise, every aspect of the work from methods of compilation and editorial procedure to the exact form of abbreviations and the principles of cross-referencing. Every fine detail of the whole work should be pondered, and every foreseeable problem carefully considered. Although much would have to be provisional in the first instance, the editor should record his conclusions in a file notebook long before work began. This could be modified as work developed, and it would eventually serve as an editorial or style manual and as a 'bible' of decisions. As a record of decisions, and of the reasons for taking or modifying them, it would be invaluable. It is not difficult to foresee some of the problems likely to confront the editor of a *DSB* and to anticipate the kind of solution that he might record in his 'bible'.

First of all there would be what is always the initial task with a reference work — that of definition. What is a Scot? Embodied in that question there are overtones of two others: where is a Scot, and when is a Scot? If the work is to be comprehensive it must take note of the earliest times as well as the most recent. So in going back to the ninth-century reign of King Kenneth MacAlpin it would often be necessary to consider the era and the location of a candidate for inclusion before deciding whether or not he or she were a Scot. A modern legal definition would not do. A definition derived from the common-sense view that James Hogg and Robert Burns are archetypal Scots could lead to the conclusion that national heroes like Sir William Wallace and King Robert the Bruce were not. I would propose a very loose working definition to be refined as compilation proceeded and experience was gained. Initially, persons to be considered for inclusion in a *DSB* should be Scottish by birth, blood, or association. And, of course, they should be dead.

A very small problem, but one that might not be ignored, provides a contrast. Many Scottish names begin with the letters 'Mc'. One McLellan might write his name in that way; another may insist that it is correct only in the form McLellan. Historically the latter is presumably the more accurate; the superior 'c' indicates a contraction and the omission of the letter 'a' from 'Mac'. Since the editor of a biographical dictionary has no licence to tinker with the form of name preferred by the individual, the distinction ought to be preserved. But think of the difficulties of checking this particular point; consider too the extra expense of the type-setting; and contemplate with apprehension the certainty of getting many of the preferred forms wrong. The solution must be to make no distinction and to use only the form with the 'c' on the base line. But the introduction to the *DSB* would need to include an explanation of the difficulty and its solution, coupled with a graceful and (it is to be hoped) acceptable apology.

That was a mild problem with a fairly easy solution. But with work of this kind the solution of a problem often produces another problem. Names again provide an example. The alphabetical ordering of names would be an inescapable feature of every part of the work. Personal names would, naturally, be placed after the surname. But unless strict control were maintained from the very moment information was received, there would inevitably be confusion about whether, say, Duncan Stewart or Stewart Duncan was the correct form. The way to eliminate this danger is at once apparent: surnames would need always to be submitted and consistently recorded in upper case letters and other names in lower. There is no ambiguity about Duncan STEWART, whether in reversed form or not. But an editorial rule should not have too many exceptions. So how should a Gaelic name like Donnchadh Ban Mac an t-Saoir (Duncan Ban MacIntyre) or a quasi-pseudonym such as The Lord General of the Army (the Earl of Leven) be treated? Furthermore a prudent editor would always want to be in possession of the full form of a name. Unless he remained alert, however, he might cheerfully place in his records a statement about (here mythically) one Angus Ian James Dougall (Knt) only to discover when time was short and the printer waiting that he did not know whether this gentleman had been dubbed Sir Angus, Sir Ian, or Sir James.

For a moment I would like to refer back almost in parenthesis, as it were, to my mention of 'alphabetical ordering'. A simple matter? But an experienced indexer would immediately ask 'word-by-word or all-through?'. That is, an order (word-by-word) in which Nicols comes after Nicol Smith and before Nicolson, or, alternatively (all-through), where Nicols precedes Nicol Smith and Nicolson. In some contexts even alphabetical ordering calls for editorial thought!

It is for the recording of decisions about a multiplicity of details like these that an editor's 'bible' is so valuable. But it also serves another purpose: that of guiding the editor in writing his introduction to the completed work. I do not think that I am being eccentric in urging the great importance of there being included in any major reference work a detailed editorial introduction describing the work's purpose, limitations, and conventions. No matter how lengthy it might be I think that this editorial statement should provide an exact answer to any question about the work that might reasonably be asked by someone consulting it — and the manner in which this information were presented (that is, perhaps, in headed sections and sub-sections, even with an index) should be such that an answer would be readily found. No reader would want to be inescapably detained by a long introduction; but everyone using the work would have the right, if in doubt, to be quickly informed of exactly what was being offered.

It would seem wise to assemble any work of this nature on computer. The computer offers the most flexible editorial facilities, the work could be constantly updated, and on computer the information remains readily available, in a way that printed volumes cannot provide. I am not an expert in such matters, and I cannot speak convincingly of kilobytes, fields, and codes. I must describe what I, as editor of a *DSB*, would require of the computer. I would want to be able to view the information as I was either storing or editing it; I would want to be able to have a print-out whenever I felt inclined; I would expect the computer to place the entries in alphabetical order, and to supply a numerical count of them at any time; and finally I would want the facility of being able to create indexes. As for typography, I suspect that no more would be required than upper- and lower-case, common punctuation marks, and a method of indicating italic type in a way that would be recognised by the printer's type-setting technology. To those of you reasonably familiar with computers this will sound naive. And so it is. But I have found it best in dealing with experts in technology who may be unfamiliar with scholarly needs — and especially with literary needs — to be simple, unambiguous, and totally explicit in describing essential requirements. The fields that would be required would be the obvious ones to receive surname, other names, titles, dates of birth and death, a descriptive word or phrase indicating the nature of the subject's achievement (poet, surgeon, politician, golfer), place of birth or association, and the like. But in addition to these obvious fields it would be necessary to have others for Gaelic names, pseudonyms, a 'floruit' date, and, of course, fields for arms, portrait, and sources — the major field being the account of the subject's life.

Using a computer would facilitate the production of the simple lists of names which — were I the editor of a *DSB* — I should regard as essential. I should look for three of these, and I should distinguish between them by the epithets 'preliminary', 'working', and 'final'. The entries in each of them would, at least initially, give no more than name, dates, an indication of the nature of the achievement, and the source of the information. 'FALCONER, William (1732–1769), poet. Royle' could be taken as a simple example.

The 'Preliminary List of Names' could, and indeed should, be compiled quickly. It should be based initially upon the many obvious published sources. There exists a very large number of books that would have to be consulted because their titles alone — if not their quality — demand it. Works by Chambers, Berg, Michel, Rattray, Steuart, such as have already been noticed, may prove to be unreliable in some details. But they would necessarily have to be scrutinised. Any Scot, no matter of how small distinction, who has been sufficiently eminent to find mention even in an insignificant biographical work would have a claim to be considered for inclusion in a *DSB*. I would expect there to be at least two thousand of these readily available reference works, and it would be very informative to discover quickly how many names for consideration they yielded. This 'Preliminary List of Names' would in due course be enlarged by names culled from specialist monographs, local newspapers, trade journals, and other similar reading. To begin with, the number of names it contained would fluctuate, perhaps violently, as the editorial process of addition and exclusion developed. Eventually this list would be refined to become the 'Working List of Names'. That list might conveniently carry rather more detail than the previous version. For instance, the nature of achievement could usefully be indicated specifically rather than with a general term: the initial classification of 'nobleman' against the name of an infamous eighteenth-century Earl of Drumlanrig being augmented by 'idiot, murderer, cannibal' — though one hopes that this might be a bizarre example. It is upon the foundation of the 'Working List of Names' that archival investigation and research work generally would be based. I would expect that a large contribution to the refining of this list would come by way of correspondence offering private information. Eventually the 'Final List of Names' would emerge, canonising, as it were, those worthies who were to be noticed by an entry in the *DSB*. I would add three comments about this plan. Firstly, the heavy reliance in the first instance on published sources should not be taken to imply that the *DSB* might actually be a mere compendium of published information; rather, I am proposing only the observance of the accepted precept for beginning research, 'first master your printed sources'. Secondly, I do not suggest that all other work on the *DSB* should be suspended until the completion of the 'Final List of Names'. Lastly, I am concerned to emphasise the value of the 'Preliminary List of Names' and to add that I believe that it should be based upon a finite number of reference works — I did mention two thousand — and that every effort should be made to create this list with all speed. It has an important role.

The 'Preliminary List of Names' would be useful in several ways. First of all it would give a very clear idea of whether the estimate — or educated guess — of some thirty thousand entries was realistic. Negotiations with potential publishers could only be conducted if there were available an acceptable, or defensible, figure of this kind.

On its accuracy as a first estimate would depend whether the work could be planned to fit comfortably into three volumes or whether, say, five or even more would be required. Also it would provide the opportunity of drawing attention to the progress of the work and of obtaining information. A copy of this list (or possibly of the 'Working List of Names', if progress had been good) could be deposited in those major libraries of the world willing to allow ready access to it by scholars, and attached to this list should be a request for information, either supplementary or corrective. My experience has been that the practice of making early drafts and first proofs open to public inspection can be very rewarding.

Another most important use of such a list is that it would allow the nature of the necessary research to be given an early estimate. Research into, say, medical archives would be facilitated from the beginning by the knowledge that there would be the names of at least fifteen hundred men and women to be considered. No doubt some of that number would, for one reason or another, not be included, while other names would present themselves. But it would be more efficient to plan an approach to medical archives and reference works supported by such a list rather than to turn to them many times – fifteen hundred times? – with single names as they occurred.

Among the problems that the editor would meet in considering names for inclusion in the 'Preliminary List' would be that of the eminent non-achiever. By 'eminent non-achiever' I refer to those who have inherited famous names or occupations, succeeding to eminent positions without achieving distinction on a purely personal basis. For example, no *DSB* could omit entries for the Dukes of Hamilton, holders of the premier Dukedom of Scotland. Similarly what is to be made of the premier Marquessate, Earldom, Viscountcy, Barony, and Baronetcy of Scotland? Undoubtedly, these styles, and most of the individual holders of them, must be noticed. But how? Also, how would one deal with any holder of high office who might not have attained any eminence apart from election to that office? It is, of course, most improper of me to imply that any holder of high office could otherwise lack distinction. But would it not present a problem?

Until the 'Working List of Names', at least, had been reasonably established and had survived keen and informed scrutiny it would be imprudent for the editor, in my view, to embark upon the actual writing of the entries. Whether the writing were to be undertaken intensively by a small team of general historians or by a much larger number of specialists it should wait upon the near completion at least of this list. Otherwise administrative complications could be expected. These would arise from the nature of the entries. They would be of virtually two kinds: those based upon research, and the others for which the facts have long been established, as with King James VI, Robert Louis Stevenson, and Ramsay MacDonald. Their lives have been so well documented that it would be impossible for even the most dedicated researcher to uncover new facts that might effect a concise entry in a *DSB*. (A good editor would, nevertheless, insist that an entry for someone such as King James, Stevenson, or MacDonald must be written in a manner as fresh as if the information were being offered for the first time.)

One final comment must be made about these three lists. That is, the knowledge that they were being compiled would certainly provoke the objection of there being no need to include entries in the *DSB* for those persons who were either represented in the *Dictionary of National Biography* or who had been the subject of a good specialist study. Alternatively, it might well be proposed with some show of reason that in such instances an entry in the *DSB* need consist of no more than adequate references to other sources. I would vehemently deny that either is acceptable. The former would produce no more than a supplement to the *Dictionary of National Biography*; the latter would result in just one more narrowly limited biographical dictionary with a bibliography of Scottish biographies. In each instance it would be a work ancillary to others. Furthermore, there would be great difficulties in planning its continuing updating, because its contents would always be dependent upon the choices of another editor and various biographers. Also the editor of this kind of *DSB* would be overwhelmed by the task of assessing new biographies as they appeared. I can see no need for such a project. But I do see a great need for a biographical dictionary of Scots that would quickly acquire a reputation, not only for including everything that might reasonably be asked of it, but also for being a good place to look for relevant, but out-of-the-way information. I would not want anyone seeking information about, say, Black Douglas to be told that there would be no point in turning to the *DSB* because Black Douglas was just famous enough for him not to have been given a full entry. Rather, I would hope that the *DSB* would come to be considered both a prime authority, and also a fruitful source of information about persons even only obscurely Scottish (perhaps like Marshal of France the Comte de Lauriston).

Another problem that would arise, where ample documentation is available, concerns the imaginative arts, and especially the creations of literary figures. The works of Sir Walter Scott provide a good example. Should they all be listed in his entry? And what of the paintings of Sir David Wilkie, the architectural works of the Adam brothers, and the vast musical canon of Sir Alexander Campbell Mackenzie? Their creations are the reason for their fame. How could they not be fully recorded? There is no simple answer. Such instances would call for shrewd editorial judgement and it is in such matters that an editor would prove his quality. But I would emphasise one thing. I have proposed a concise form of entry; that is, an entry which is factual rather than interpretative. I do not propose a concise dictionary. That would be quite a different thing. I would expect many of the entries, especially those devoted to men and women of great affairs, to be extensive. Yet it seems very probable that more than half of the thirty thousand entries (if that were indeed the number) would be short and would, not infrequently, consist of but one or two lines (no more are required even for a celebrity like Maggie Dickson who was hanged at Edinburgh in 1728, but who was revived by the jolting of the hearse over the cobbles and survived to have many children!).

One of the justifications for a *DSB*, as I have claimed, would be the great achievements of the emigrant Scot. The numerous Caledonian Societies and St Andrews Societies throughout the world today witness to the tenacity with which the emigrant Scot preserves a feeling of national identity. Nevertheless Scots have fully integrated themselves with the peoples among whom they have gone to live and they have had children. If those children became eminent how are they to be treated by the editor of a *DSB*? The Italian foreign minister, Sidney Sonnino, distinguished himself at the Paris Peace Conference in 1919 because of his command of English. He apparently learned his fluent English from his Scottish mother. Should he be given an entry? Perhaps not. But what should be done (to take as an example the family already noticed) with the Greigs? Grand Admiral Sir Samuel Greig was born a Scot, whatever his later nationality may have been. But his son, Admiral Alexis Greig, and his grandson, General Samuel Greig, were surely Russians? Yet I would find it difficult to allow myself to be persuaded that their exploits have no place in any account of Sir Samuel. Furthermore it would seem to me fitting that they should be given more than a mere mention. I would argue that there is a strong case for giving each of them a separate entry. Two separate entries cross-referenced to that of Sir Samuel Greig would be a very convenient way of dealing with them (and others like them). Thus, it would be possible to give an adequate amount of information about each of them without swelling Sir Samuel's entry; the significance of their inclusion in a *DSB* would be marked in a proper manner; and, perhaps most important of all, it would be a convenient way of ensuring that their names appeared in the appropriate indexes. It is precisely the kind of information that anyone consulting a *DSB* has no absolute right to expect but the presence of which would enhance the reputation of the work. Perhaps entries for the eminent (but technically non-Scottish) descendants of emigrant Scots might be distinguished by an asterisk, or some comparable symbol?

I earlier mentioned that correspondence would bring private information and for this hopeful assumption I can advance no evidence at all beyond instinct and experience. I think that once it were known that the work was in progress the editor of the *DSB* would be inundated by information about unnoticed Scottish achievers. It seems certain that descendants would draw his attention to the unremarked founder of a present-day great bank, or would reveal that an ancestor raised a regiment to fight in the American Civil War, or would produce evidence that a revolutionary design for a ship's stabiliser was the work of a Scottish relative. It would need no more than a very brief circular letter to alert the members of all the numerous, world-wide, societies formed to preserve Scottish associations. A very small initial effort in making the projected work known would be self-generating. A proportion of the unsolicited information would prove to have little immediate value. But I suspect that much of it would be as treasure-trove. Although, of course, there would be some humorists. One such might be the man who demonstrated that Dante was really a Scot. His father, so the story went, was a Jute merchant of Dundee named Alec Gair. He emigrated to Italy, where the son was born. He was named Alec after his father. But his Italian friends found his surname difficult to pronounce and eventually turned it into Ghairi. So he became known as Alec Ghairi. And as Macaulay's schoolboy undoubtedly knew, Dante's surname was indeed Alighieri.

To conclude on a more serious note, I would take this opportunity of recording a plea for the creation of national biographical archives. Thanks to the computer, it is now possible to record, classify, and make accessible an amount of material that no reference library could readily contain. Since Scots have so often led the way in the past, I suggest that a beginning be made with them. I would like to see all the information gathered for a *DSB* left permanently on computer, and constantly updated. And I would like to see a clearly defined movement on a national scale to ensure that the names, with relevant biographical information, of Scottish achievers are entered while they are still flourishing. Other countries, as has so often happened, might then follow the Scottish example. I think posterity would approve.

JAMES B. MISENHEIMER, Jnr, is Professor of English at Indiana State University, where he served as Chairman of the Department of English from 1972 to 1978. Professor Misenheimer is a noted Johnson scholar, and a Vice-President of The Johnson Society of London and The Charles Lamb Society, and has also published widely on Charles Lamb and on the prose of the Romantic Period. For sixteen years he was the American Editor of the Modern Humanities Reseach Association's *Annual Bibliography of English Language and Literature.* Among the numerous awards he has received is the coveted Caleb Mills Award for Distinguished Teaching.

Dr Johnson, Warren Cordell, and the love of books

JAMES B. MISENHEIMER, Jnr

In 1644, in his brilliant defence of the freedom of the press known as the *Areopagitica*, John Milton defined a good book as 'the precious life-blood of a master-spirit, embalmed and treasured up on purpose to a life beyond life'. He was here speaking in defence of books as one aspect of his argument against censorship, though he could just as easily have been pronouncing the credo for bibliophiles the world over; for if indeed a good book is 'the precious life-blood of a master-spirit', it is deserving of the kind of attention stemming not only from scholarly interest, but also from the love, the care, and the respect sometimes manifest in an ardent collector, eager to nurture and to cherish in one place a portion of the cultural and intellectual legacy that is ours.

From our study of literary history, we know that not all great authors have been great collectors, just as not all great collectors have been great authors. We think of Sir Robert Cotton, but for whose efforts at collecting we might never have come to recognise and share in the glories of the Anglo Saxon epic *Beowulf* or in the productions of the Pearl Poet. His collection is his great claim to fame. But we also think of Coleridge and De Quincey, two of the greatest representatives of English romanticism and also two of the most notorious borrowers of books on record. You will recall Lamb's acerbic references to Coleridge as an example of those who borrow in the famous essay 'The Two Races of Men'. Coleridge often scribbled in books that were not his own, and De Quincey cut out with the scissors favourite or needed passages, seldom concerned with the sensitivities of the book owner as he did so. Samuel Johnson, from childhood, possessed an inveterate love of books. He was born above his father's bookshop in Lichfield, and from his earliest years Samuel had a profound respect for books as both physical objects and repositories of knowledge.

Indeed, in the early 1750s, when Johnson was writing as the Rambler, he referred in essay No. 92 to Boileau, who Johnson says 'justly remarks, that the books which have stood the test of time, and been admired through all the changes which the mind of man has suffered from the various revolutions of knowledge . . . have a better claim to our regard than any modern can boast, because the long continuance of their reputation proves that they are adequate to our faculties, and agreeable to nature'.[1]

One of Johnson's many statements regarding love of books as an integral part of being a fully developed human being – a statement similar to Boileau's, though it begins in analogy – appears in a letter to his young friend Hester Maria Thrale, written on 28 August 1780, as follows:

> It is well for me that a Lady so celebrated as Miss Thrale can find time to write to me. I will recompense your condescension with a maxim. Never treat old friends with neglect however easily you may find new. There is a tenderness which seems the the meer growth of time, but which is in [fact] the effect [of] many combinations; those with whom we have shared enjoyments, we remember with pleasure, those with whom we have shared sorrow, we remember with tenderness. You must already have begun to observe that you love a book . . . that you have had a great part of your life, because it brings a great part of your life back to your view.[2]

Johnson's love of books expressed itself primarily, of course, through his choice of writing as his profession. At no time in his life did he have at his command large sums of money which would have allowed him to become a full-fledged collector of books in the modern sense. But his intense interest in the profession of authorship led him to a deep sense of responsibility for what books say and for how they can influence human thought and conduct. It is

1. Samuel Johnson, *The Rambler*, No. 92, *The Yale Edition of the Works of Samuel Johnson*, edited by W. J. Bate and A. B. Strauss (New Haven, 1969), IV, p.122.

2. R. W. Chapman (editor), *The Letters of Samuel Johnson* (Oxford, 1952), II, p. 399.

true that Johnson did not relish the discipline of writing. It is also true that he was his own harshest critic. Nevertheless, he *knew* that he had something worthwhile to say about the art of living, and though as he told the King no man is obliged to do all that he can, he devoted himself professionally to contributions to literary genres almost too numerous to count.

Paul Fussell has pointed out in his book *Samuel Johnson and the Life of Writing* that Johnson 'worked in tragedy, biography, the periodical essay, the oriental tale, the travel book, the political tract, the critical essay, and the book review; in the oration, the sermon, the letter, the prayer, the dedication, the preface, the legal brief, and the petition to royalty; in the poetic satire, the Horatian ode, the elegy, the theatrical prologue and epilogue, the song, the Anacreontic lyric, the epigram, and the epitaph'.[3] Johnson wrote from the belief that authorship is among the most intensely personal of professions. It verges on confessional and hence lays the author's soul open to the scrutiny of the world. Thus his respect for books takes the form of a strong devotion to his profession; and though he owned many books, he did not always take time to attend to them as he ought, nor did he consider himself a collector. It was his fervent hope that men and women would be affected by the instruction of literature well written. In the *Rambler*, No. 57, he writes: 'I am always pleased when I see literature made useful, and scholars descending from that elevation, which, as it raises them above common life, must likewise hinder them from beholding the ways of men otherwise than in a cloud of bustle and confusion'.[4]

Thus it is, then, that Milton's definition of a good book as the 'precious life-blood of a master-spirit' is a definition universal, replete with implications and ramifications for all who cultivate a life of the mind. And it is a definition that undergirds perhaps one of the greatest collections of books in twentieth-century America, the Cordell Collection of Dictionaries at Indiana State University, in which Dr Johnson is so fully represented.

'The embalming and treasuring up on purpose of a life beyond life' was begun a number of years ago by Warren Cordell of Chicago when his interest in old dictionaries began to take the form of

3. Paul Fussell, *Samuel Johnson and the Life of Writing* (New York, 1971), II, pp. 38–39.

4. *The Rambler*, No. 57, *Yale Edition*, III, p. 305.

collecting. Mr Cordell, who died in 1980, once remarked that the collecting of old dictionaries was not the result of 'logical appraisal' but rather 'an emotional course of action' that he had never bothered to examine too closely. Having grown up, like Johnson, among books, he was eventually led — or driven — by an unusual desire to acquire thousands of old dictionaries. He had early been fascinated by words — by the magic and power of language; and he on one occasion confessed the possibility that among the hidden recesses of the dictionary bibliomaniac's mind is the belief that physical acquisition of a book is tantamount to the mental acquisition and intellectual assimilation of its contents.

Mr Cordell always insisted that he was not a scholar. He was, at least on the surface, a very successful business executive whose success eventually permitted him an avocation in the world of books that by far transcends and surpasses the professed scholarly interests and research of many who are primarily professional and scholarly. And when a flash flood from a cloudburst began pouring into the area of his home where his dictionary collection was shelved, he approached his *alma mater*, Indiana State University, about providing a home for these volumes in its new library. He said that since this new library was to be constructed only a few miles from his birthplace, which was a flat over his father's grocery store, the opportunity of giving his collection a special residence in the university seemed to provide a poetic ending. The arrangements at Indiana State's Cunningham Memorial Library exceeded even Mr Cordell's greatest expectations when it was decided that a special Cordell Room to house the collection would be planned as part of the rare books section. And the good fortune continued when a grant from the National Endowment for the Humanities was obtained which matched the value of Mr Cordell's first gift of four hundred and fifty-three dictionaries, a sum that permitted significant additional acquisitions, repairs, and cataloguing and use of the collection. The University's own programme for gradual improvement through a regular acquisition fund meant, moreover, that the Cordell Collection would remain alive and retain its place among the world's best collections of dictionaries.

The current status of the Collection would no doubt be of special interest to you before we examine further some of the processes and techniques of collecting that Mr Cordell followed.

The Warren N. and Suzanne B. Cordell Collection of Dictionaries, totalling now more than eight thousand volumes, represents virtually the entire spectrum of Western lexicography from the manuscript period to the present day. It also includes a sizeable representation of non-Western language dictionaries. From the beginning, however, emphasis has been placed on collecting pre-1900 English language dictionaries and English bilingual dictionaries important in the development of English and American lexicography. The Collection includes complete or nearly complete runs of almost every major English language dictionary published since Robert Cawdrey's *A Table Alphabeticall* appeared in 1604. For example, the Collection boasts more than two hundred different editions and issues of Samuel Johnson's *A Dictionary of the English Language* plus splendid copies of the 'Chesterfield' and 'Non-Chesterfield' issues of the 1747 *Plan* in quarto and the 1755 octavo edition of the *Plan*. The Collection also includes every known edition of Nathan Bailey's *Etymological English Dictionary*, volumes I and II. Many copies in the Collection are unique, i.e., they represent the only recorded copies of a particular edition or issue of a work. Some are distinctive in other ways, as, for example, Peter Roget's personal copy of the first edition of his *Thesaurus*, with extensive corrections, revisions, and annotations throughout in his own hand.

While early English language dictionaries continue to be the focal point of the Cordell Collection, increasing attention in recent years has been given to the collecting of major Renaissance and pre-1800 foreign language dictionaries, for these too were important in the development of English lexicography. Because of the generally high cost and relative scarcity of early modern European lexicons, it is doubtful that the Library will ever aim at being as comprehensive in this area as it is in the area of English and American lexicography. Nevertheless, the Cordell Collection includes a rather impressive representation of most of the key Renaissance and pre-1800 foreign language dictionaries. In some cases, it is outstanding. For example, its twenty-five different editions of Ambrosio Calepino's *Dictionarium*, perhaps the most influential lexicon of the Renaissance, rank it among the finest such holdings in the world. By comparison, the British Library and the *Bibliothèque Nationale* record only twenty copies each of Calepino's work.

While emphasis has been placed on strengthening the Collection's pre-1900 dictionary holdings, the twentieth century has not been entirely forgotten or neglected. Of the more than eight thousand volumes in the Collection, approximately twenty-five per cent were published after 1900. The number and variety of twentieth-century dictionaries is, however, staggering, and the limited resources of the Library have made it impossible to collect either aggressively or comprehensively in this period. This is not to say that the Library undervalues the importance of twentieth-century dictionaries. Quite the contrary! But the line had to be drawn somewhere, and it was decided early on that it would be wisest to concentrate initially on rare and early dictionaries. As it becomes increasingly more difficult, for whatever reasons, to fill gaps in our pre-1900 holdings, the Library will likely turn more attention to the collection of post-1900 dictionaries.

In recent years the scope of the Collection has broadened to include not only dictionaries but the papers of distinguished dictionary makers. In 1977, the Library acquired the papers of Mitford Mathews of the University of Chicago, one of the foremost American lexicographers of the twentieth century. The Mathews Papers constitute a rich source for the study of how a lexicographer collects and uses definitions in compiling a dictionary. Efforts are underway to acquire similar collections to enhance the study of lexicography at Indiana State University.

To inform the book world about the Cordell Collection, a *Short Title Catalogue,* compiled by Paul S. Koda, now of the University of North Carolina, was published in 1975 with funds from the National Endowment for the Humanities. This limited edition of 500 copies was distributed free of charge, and the supply has long since been exhausted. A new catalogue, entitled *The Warren N. and Suzanne B. Cordell Collection of Rare and Early Dictionaries, ca. 1400–1900,* by Robert K. O'Neill, is in preparation. This catalogue will include full titles in most cases, collations, including signature collations, notes, provenance, reference, entry numbers, indexes, and other bibliographical aids. It will be published in two volumes by G. K. Hall, Boston, Massachusetts. The first, entitled *English Language Dictionaries 1604–1900,* should appear in print towards the end of 1981. Volume II, *English Bilingual and Foreign Language Dictionaries,* should follow in about two years.

Since the initial gift was made by Warren Cordell in 1969, the Collection has grown in number, in scope, and in depth beyond anything either Mr Cordell or the University had envisioned. The principal force behind this growth was Warren Cordell himself. Not only did he personally donate more than seventy-five per cent of the volumes in the Collection, but he worked tirelessly to promote the Collection. To this end he was amazingly successful. Through his efforts, for example, the antiquarian book trade in North America and in England has by and large come to identify dictionary collecting with the Cordell Collection. J. Clark-Hall's *Catalogue Eighteen: 'Harmless Drudgery', Johnson and the Dictionary*, contains the following dedication:

> We would like to pay tribute to Dr. Warren N. Cordell, who died suddenly on the 5th January, 1980 and to whom we owe a great deal of our present interest in the Dictionaries. We dedicate this catalogue to a remarkable man whose collection of Dictionaries, housed at Indiana State University, is very possibly the greatest in the world, and whose enthusiasm for his subject *was* the greatest.

Numerous bookdealers, often at financial sacrifice to themselves, have taken pains in the past decade to direct dictionaries to the Cordell Collection, in large measure out of respect for Warren Cordell and for his work.

What therefore does the loss of Warren Cordell mean to the future of the Cordell Collection? Clearly, his generosity, his vision, his enthusiasm, and his knowledge will be greatly missed. But the Collection he founded has taken on a life of its own. This was his express purpose. Moreover, the University and the Cordell family are firmly committed to the enhancement of the Collection, so that an already great collection will become even greater.

But the Collection would never have become reality in its present unique form, had an unusually deep and rich love of books not possessed this man who sought and found his avocation far from the madding crowd of big business.

The private collecting of old English dictionaries is unusual, Mr Cordell once pointed out, because it differs so much in scope from collecting the works of a single author. This difference is even greater, he emphasised, when the term 'old English dictionaries' is interpreted broadly to include all kinds of dictionary, all different editions, early multi-lingual dictionaries including English, and the early Latin and Greek dictionaries that contributed to the development of the English language. Such a full-scale interpretation would have set the Collection's early goal at considerably more than five thousand dictionaries published across a period of five centuries. But Mr Cordell knew that unless a definite category or area of collection can be described, the Collection area will continue to expand as the collector's appetite grows and as bookdealers offer associated items of interest, so that the collector must exhibit considerable discipline to keep his collection instincts within appropriate bounds.

He directed his efforts to old dictionaries without troubling himself initially as to goals and purpose. Among his initial acquisitions were Webster's 1806 and 1828 editions, though for some reason Worcester's dictionaries eluded him for several years. His first acquisition of a Worcester dictionary, when finally it came, led him to a crucial reappraisal of his goals as a collector. This quarto edition of Worcester contained 'A Catalogue of English Dictionaries' — a seven-page list of three hundred and ninety-eight lexicographical works by nearly that number of lexicographers. As he studied Worcester's Catalogue, he for the first time grasped how many English lexicographers there had been, the many different kinds of dictionary, and the magnitude of work that would be involved if he held to his desire to acquire all editions instead of just first editions. He, of course, used other lists as well for gauging his progress, including those from Starnes and Noyes's *English Dictionaries from Cawdrey to Johnson*, Starnes's *Renaissance Dictionaries,* and Alston's bibliography of regular English dictionaries. Later, Hayashi's list of English dictionary first editions was helpful, although by then Mr Cordell's own sources were nearly as complete and in some cases permitted him to offer Hayashi corrections. But the Worcester list and those acquired later made him fully aware of the optimism required to undertake the ambitious programme of collecting so many old dictionaries.

As Warren Cordell became increasingly more absorbed in collecting old dictionaries, he recognised the need to set specific goals, or, to use his expression, to take the rifle rather than the shotgun approach.[5] His first aim was to assemble the finest and most comprehensive collection of old English and American English dictionaries in the United States. To identify pre-1900 English language dictionaries, he used Robin Alston's *A Bibliography of the English Language.* He set out after as many 'Alstons' as he could acquire, with the avowed pur-

5. Warren Cordell to Earl Tannenbaum, 20 January 1971. Cordell Correspondence File, Department of Rare Books and Special Collections, Cunningham Memorial Library, Indiana State University. All correspondence hereafter cited is to be found in this file; hence a location statement will not be repeated.

pose to collect every edition of every Alston title possible. 'It became an intriguing challenge', he wrote, 'to get what I choose to call a "clean sweep" of all editions'.[6] Certain titles were, for all practical purposes, impossible to collect in every edition. For example, Alston recorded only one extant copy of the 1604, 1609, and 1617 editions and only two copies of the 1613 edition of Robert Cawdrey's *A Table Alphabeticall*, the first English language dictionary. But for many and perhaps most of the Alston titles, a 'clean sweep' was a distinct possibility.

Since Alston recorded not only various editions and issues of pre-1800 English dictionary titles but also locations, Cordell was able to identify major institutional holders. To his surprise, he found in 1967 that no single library in either Britain or the United States was exceptionally strong numerically in Alston holdings. The British Museum was first, with one hundred and seventy-two out of a possible three hundred and fifty-three editions, followed by Oxford, with one hundred and sixty-three. Only five other libraries recorded more Alstons than Cordell's personal total of sixty-seven.[7] To be sure, this was a quantitative rather than a qualitative comparison, and Cordell recognised this. Nevertheless, his findings showed that his original objective to assemble the finest collection of early dictionaries in the United States was clearly within reach. It seemed to Cordell that few libraries were strongly committed to improving their dictionary holdings. Consequently, he began even to consider a more ambitious goal, namely, establishing the Cordell Collection as the finest collection of its kind anywhere. He pursued Alstons aggressively, though not to the exclusion of other dictionaries. By early 1969, he had increased his holdings to one hundred and nineteen, surpassing all but the British Museum and Oxford.[8] He finally passed the British Museum in August 1970 with the acquisition of twelve Alstons from the Gene Freeman Collection.[9]

6. Warren Cordell to Paul Koda, 22 July 1971.

7. Warren Cordell to Elvis J. Stahr, 25 January 1967. The other five in descending order were Yale, Harvard, National Library of Wales, New York Public Library, and Chicago. See Cordell letter to Fred W. Hanes, 27 March 1969, for revised figures.

8. Warren Cordell to Fred W. Hanes, 10 March 1969.

9. Warren Cordell to Gene Freeman, 25 August 1970. It should be noted that Cordell's figures were drawn exclusively from Alston, and therefore did not include possible additions to the holdings of the BM or Oxford since Alston's survey.

In his pursuit of Alstons, Cordell concentrated on two lexicographers above all – Nathan Bailey and Samuel Johnson. He was determined to make his collection of dictionaries by these two great eighteenth-century lexicographers second to none, and he spared neither time nor money in this quest. He was after nothing less than a 'clean sweep'.

Nathan Bailey was the most popular lexicographer in England throughout most of the eighteenth century. His *Universal Etymological English Dictionary* went through thirty-three editions, not including variants, between 1721 and 1802.[10] A supplementary volume, the so-called 'second' volume, was issued in seven editions between 1727 and 1776. In addition to these octavo volumes, Bailey produced a folio dictionary entitled *Dictionarium Britannicum,* published in 1730 and again in 1736, considerably revised and enlarged. Samuel Johnson used an interleaved copy of the 1730 *Dictionarium Britannicum* as a repository for his notes while compiling his own dictionary. Bailey produced one other dictionary, an octavo volume entitled *Dictionarium Domesticum,* which appeared in 1736 with no subsequent editions issued. The *Dictionarium Rusticum, Urbanicum et Botanicum* of 1704, sometimes attributed to Bailey, is now generally credited to John Worlidge (*fl.* 1669–1698).

Cordell's appetite for Baileys was voracious, indeed, omnivorous. He went after any Bailey edition available, not just those he lacked. As early as 1969 he was issuing instructions to bookdealers to buy for him any Bailey that turned up.[11] At the time of his death, he had accumulated at his home in Highland Park, Illinois, a total of one hundred and three copies of Bailey's *Universal Etymological English Dictionary.* These were in addition to the eighty-seven copies of this work already in the Cordell Collection at Indiana State University.

10. The numbering of the Bailey dictionaries is a bit puzzling. No copies of a 'twelfth', or 'nineteenth', or a 'twenty-eighth' edition have ever been discovered, and the omission of these editions in the sequence is probably due to a simple case of misnumbering. There are two thirteenth editions (London, 1747, and London, 1749), and two twelfth editions (London, 1763, and London, 1764).

　　The last numbered edition is the thirtieth, but there were also a one and-twentieth edition (London, 1766), a twenty-first edition (London, 1770), and yet another twenty-first edition (London, 1775); a twenty-fourth edition (London, 1776), and a four-and-twentieth edition (London, 1782), a twenty-fifth (London, 1783), and a five-and-twentieth edition (London, 1790): hence the total of thirty-three separate issues rather than the thirty often reported.

11. T. G. Morley to Warren Cordell, 25 February 1969.

Needless to say, Cordell's pursuit of Baileys had a significant impact on their market price. When he began his quest, later editions of Bailey's *Etymological Dictionary* in good condition were selling for between six and ten pounds.[12] These same items presently command between forty and fifty pounds.[13]

There was a bibliographic purpose to this apparent obsession with Baileys. Like many popular eighteenth-century English works, some editions of Bailey were issued by more than one group of booksellers. Ordinarily, only the publisher's imprint on the title page was altered. These changes were usually slight, sometimes involving no more than the substitution of one name for another in a long list of names. Variants of Bailey, therefore, often go undetected, and only a close examination and comparison with other copies is likely to reveal them. By pursuing Baileys so aggressively, Cordell was able to turn up several previously unrecorded variants in addition to securing copies of all the known editions and issues. Such a complete[14] collection in one place greatly facilitates the work of the bibliographer or lexicographer interested in studying Bailey. Moreover, it provides an important source for the study of the history of printing and publishing in the eighteenth century. Occasionally, it yields unexpected benefits. For some time there has been some question whether the 'Nat.' in Bailey's name stood for Nathan or Nathaniel. The *DNB* gives both. The Cordell Collection includes two copies of Bailey's *Dictionarium Britannicum* in which the dedication is signed 'George Gordon, Nat. Bailey'. But the Collection also houses a variant copy in which the dedication is signed 'Nathan Bailey. George Gordon'. The appearance of Bailey's full name in this copy would seem to clear up the matter.

Although Nathan Bailey's *Etymological Dictionary* may have been the most popular eighteenth-century English dictionary, Samuel Johnson's *A Dictionary of the English Language* was the most important and most enduring. It is fitting, therefore, that Dr Johnson's great work, called by some 'the most amazing, enduring and endearing, one-man feat in the field of lexicography',[15] should occupy the

12. Warren Cordell to Earl Tannenbaum, 22 April 1971.

13. See J. Clarke-Hall Catalogue, No. 15 (1978).

14. Several variants are still lacking.

15. John Carter to Percy H. Muir, *Printing and the Mind of Man* (London, 1967), p. 121.

position of greatest prominence in the Cordell Collection. In Dr Cordell's initial gift of dictionaries to Indiana State University in 1969, there was a total of one hundred and two separate editions and issues of the *Dictionary* — thirty-four eighteenth-century editions and sixty-eight nineteenth-century editions. This compared with twenty-two pre-1800 Johnsons at Oxford and twenty at the British Museum as of 1966. At present, as already remarked, the Cordell Collection includes more than two hundred different pre-1900 editions and issues of the *Dictionary* plus all three issues of the *Plan.*

The number of editions and issues of Dr Johnson's masterpiece can be confusing and perhaps even a bit misleading. The first edition of the *Dictionary* appeared in two folio volumes in 1755. Before Johnson's death in 1784, four more two-volume folio editions were issued, only one of which, the fourth (London, 1773), had been considerably revised by Johnson. A quarto edition was printed in Dublin in 1775. There were seven numbered abstracted editions published in octavo between 1756 and 1783, not including variants. The first Dublin edition was published by the Ewings in octavo in 1758. Thus, the number of editions printed in Johnson's lifetime was not especially large. Nevertheless, Dr Johnson's impact on lexicography was quickly recognised, and his *Dictionary* became the benchmark by which the quality of other dictionaries was measured.

As a result, there began to appear soon after Johnson's death a steady stream of dictionaries which purported to be supplements to or to be based upon, modelled upon, or otherwise indebted to his *Dictionary.* While many of these editions were closely related to the original Johnsons, many more were not. Some, particularly the miniature variety popular towards the end of the eighteenth century and throughout the nineteenth century, bore little or no resemblance to the original Johnsons. These lexicons, however, have been traditionally catalogued by libraries as Johnsons. Moreover, they are of historical, bibliographical, and philological interest to Johnson scholars, particularly those whose research involves the tracing of Johnson's impact on lexicography in the nineteenth century. For these reasons, Warren Cordell sought to collect every 'Johnson' available, however questionable its lineage.

The decision to collect Johnsons was not an automatic one for Warren Cordell, however. He learned early on that Johnsons would be considerably more costly to collect than Baileys or other English language dictionaries — one of the inevitable consequences of the enduring interest in early Johnson editions. Though he was a sucessful business executive who enjoyed a very comfortable income in the early 1960s, he was not a wealthy man. With four college-bound children, Cordell had to consider seriously the cost factors in pursuing his collecting interests. By his own admission, it took him awhile to train himself to accept the prices it would be necessary to pay if he were going to collect dictionaries, especially Johnsons, vigorously. He turned down the first 1755 Johnson set offered to him at the price of fourteen hundred dollars.[16] But Cordell's eventual decision to pay the prices necessary to achieve his goals was probably never seriously in doubt. He had been bitten by the book collecting bug, and for this traumatic disease there is no known cure.

It would be greatly remiss of me to discuss Warren Cordell's magnificent achievement without paying credit to those who so greatly helped to make this achievement possible – namely, the antiquarian bookdealers in North America and Europe. Cordell was always the first to acknowledge his great debt to the many men and women of the book trade who participated in the building of the Cordell Collection. 'Without their friendly help and cooperation', he once wrote, 'my efforts would have been futile'.[17]

Indeed, he was attracted to book collecting for the fellowship of others who shared his love of books as much as for the physical possession of books or the thrill of making a 'clean sweep'. He visited bookshops at every opportunity and passed countless hours sharing news, anecdotes, and bits of knowledge with his bibliophilic friends. His enthusiasm for dictionaries was contagious, and his many friends in the book trade often took great pains – sometimes at personal financial sacrifice, as mentioned earlier – to direct a key dictionary to the Cordell Collection. Warren Cordell always appreciated this help and friendship. In the Foreword to the Cordell *STC*, he wrote '. . . I am extremely grateful, not only for their help, but also for their giving me the time to know them and share our mutual interests, not just in scholarly works but in world developments and our philosophies on life'.[18]

16. Paul S. Koda (compiler), *A Short-Title Catalogue of the Warren N. and Suzanne B. Cordell Collection of Dictionaries 1475–1900* (Terre Haute, 1975), p. xiv.

17. Cordell *STC*, p. xvi.

18. Cordell *STC*, p.xvi,

It should not, then, seem strange that so many volumes that *are* Dr Johnson's dictionary should have taken up residence as one of the most vital segments of the renowned Cordell Collection at Indiana State University. For Warren Cordell, in his avocation, and Samuel Johnson, in his profession, though separated by two centuries, shared a love and a respect for books and for the learning that books can represent. I like to think of how Johnson might have regarded Warren Cordell as a man of unique parts whose love of books – indeed, whose unusual devotion to the lexicographical portion of the great humanistic tradition – makes it possible, through his collection, for scholars and humanists from all parts of the world to have access to segments of our intellectual heritage which otherwise could have remained inaccessible and undiscovered for decades to come. In his 'Idler' essay, No. 91, Johnson has remarked that 'many useful and valuable books lie buried in shops and libraries, unknown and unexamined, unless some lucky compiler opens them by chance, and finds an easy spoil of wit and learning'.[19] Warren Cordell was, of course, a compiler in his own right. And his service to the scholarly world, through his collection, has proved extraordinary, and will continue to prove so.

It is not only appropriate but also reassuring to see that Johnson's *Dictionary,* in its numerous editions and issues, forms so integral a part of the Cordell Collection. Johnson was the most highly respected man of letters of his day, and his salutations to his friends and to his reading public resound in particular throughout his letters and his essays to reveal the priority of emphasis that he placed upon books and their influence. Even just a few select passages from his letters underscore the profound respect – and need – that he felt:

> 1 For example, on 8 December 1763 he wrote to his new friend James Boswell, who was studying law in Utrecht: 'At least resolve, while you remain in any settled residence, to spend a certain number of hours every day amongst your books ... If you can but kindle in your mind any strong desire, if you can but keep predominant any wish for some particular excellence or attainment, the gusto of imagination will break away'.[20]

19. Samuel Johnson, 'The Idler', No. 91, *The Yale Edition of the Works of Samuel Johnson,* edited by W. J. Bate, John M. Bullitt, and L. F. Powell (New Haven, 1963), II, p. 282.

20. *Letters,* I, p. 165.

2 In a sense, even more moving is a brief exhortation to his black manservant Francis Barber, written on 25 September 1770 when Barber was away from London: 'Let me know what English books you read for your entertainment. You can never be wise unless you love reading'.[21]

3 To Hester Maria Thrale, or Queeney, mentioned earlier, the daughter of Mr and Mrs Henry Thrale of brewery fame, he wrote on 18 July 1780: 'You, my Love, are now in the time of flood, your powers are hourly encreasing, do not lose the time. When you are alone read diligently, they who do not read can have nothing to think, and little to say'.[22]

4 To Boswell, then in Edinburgh, on 2 July 1776 he wrote: 'To hear that you have not opened your boxes of books is very offensive. The examination and arrangement of so many volumes might have afforded you an amusement very seasonable at present, and useful for the whole of life. I am, I confess, very angry that you manage yourself so ill . . .'[23]

5 And again to Boswell, only four days later: 'Let me know whether I have not sent you a pretty library. There are, perhaps, many books among them which you never need read through; but there are none which it is not proper for you to know, and sometimes to consult'.[24]

6 Again to Queeney on 24 July 1783: 'Your account of your time gives me pleasure. Never lose the habit of reading, nor ever suffer yourself to acquiesce in total vacuity . . . If ever therefore you catch yourself contentedly and placidly doing nothing . . . break away from the snare, find your book or your needle, or snatch the broom from the maid'.[25]

7 And finally to another young friend, Jane Langton, on 10 May 1784: 'I am glad, my Dear, to see that you write so well, and hope that you mind your pen, your book, and your needle, for they are all necessary. Your books will give you knowledge, and make you respected . . .'[26]

As we read Johnson's advice to Jane Langton, we are aware of the

21. *Letters*, I, p. 245.

22. *Letters*, II, p. 381.

23. *Letters*, II, p. 145.

24. *Letters*, II, pp. 146–47.

25. *Letters*, III, p. 53.

26. *Letters*, III, p. 162.

date of this letter, 10 May 1784, since his death was only seven months away. 'Your books will give you knowledge, and make you respected' – these words could be said to comprise a very fitting valediction to the lives of both Dr Johnson and Warren Cordell.

We turn, then, briefly, once again, to the recognition of Johnson's abiding regard for the profession of authorship – a regard which informed his love of the world of books when books were at their best. His idealism was regularly tempered by his firm grasp of reality. Thus in 'Idler' essay No. 85 he offers this admixture of what he wishes on the one hand and what he acknowledges on the other:

> One of the peculiarities which distinguish the present age is the multiplication of books . . .
>
> How much happiness or knowledge is advanced by this multitude of authors, it is not very easy to decide.
>
> He that teaches us anything which we knew not before, is undoubtedly to be reverenced as a master. He that conveys knowledge by more pleasing ways, may very properly be loved as a benefactor; and he that supplies life with innocent amusement, will be certainly caressed as a pleasing companion.[27]

But Johnson often pricked the illusion of others who saw writers as residing in worlds apart from common life, and his statements in this regard remind us of his own days in Grub Street which have their poignant corollary in Warren Cordell's earliest dreams of collecting. Thus in 'Idler' No. 51:

> Of men, as of everything else, we must judge according to our knowledge. When we see of a hero only his battles, or of a writer only his books, we have nothing to allay our ideas of their greatness. We consider the one only as the guardian of his country, and the other only as the instructor of mankind. We have neither opportunity nor motion to examine the minuter parts of their lives, or the less apparent pecularities of their characters; we name them with habitual respect, and forget, what we still continue to know, that they are men like other mortals.[28]

Even in the face of such reality, however, it was at times impossible

---

27. 'The Idler', No. 85, *Yale Edition*, II, p. 264.

28. 'The Idler', No. 51, *Yale Edition*, II, p. 159.

for Johnson not to set himself apart, as it were. Boswell records this telling instance as proof: '[Johnson] told Sir Joshua Reynolds, that once when he dined in a numerous company of booksellers, where the room being small, the head of the table, at which he sat, was almost close to the fire, he persevered in suffering a great deal of inconvenience from the heat, rather than quit his place, and let one of them sit above him'.[29] Surely, lurking somewhere nearby, was the spirit of Warren Cordell, waiting to be born.

29. James Boswell, *Life of Johnson*, edited by George Birkbeck Hill, revised and enlarged by Lawrence F. Powell (Oxford, 1934–50), III, p. 311.

ROBERT LATHAM is an Honorary Fellow of Magdalene College, Cambridge, and until 1982 was Pepys Librarian there. In 1970–83 he published, with the late Professor William Matthews, the first full edition of Pepys's diary in eleven volumes. Robert Latham is a Fellow of the British Academy and in 1973 was appointed CBE. He is now at work on an edition of Pepys's office diaries for the Navy Records Society.

Pepys and his editors

R. C. LATHAM

I have chosen to talk tonight about the methods used by myself and my colleagues in the new edition of Pepys. But it will be necessary as well as proper to say something first about the work of our predecessors.

Three men preceded us as editors – Lord Braybrooke, who brought out the first edition in 1825 (and afterwards others); Mynors Bright, who published a fresh transcription in the 1870s; and H. B. Wheatley, who was responsible for the big edition in ten volumes in the 1890s. Between them these three established the fame of the diary. They were very different men: Braybrooke, a dilettante aristocrat; Bright, a Cambridge classics don; and Wheatley, a London antiquarian. But their editions were very similar, and had a certain amount of editorial material in common. There was in fact no fundamental change in the editorial design until the new edition.

The manuscript of the diary had, by the terms of Pepys's will, come into the possession of his old college, Magdalene Cambridge, in 1724, along with the rest of his library, where it remained virtually unnoticed for close on a hundred years. It was written almost entirely in a shorthand no one had attempted to transcribe, but the publication of the diary of his friend John Evelyn in 1818 drew attention to it, and the decision was made to publish it.

At this time Magdalene was in certain respects a patrimony of the Nevilles of Audley End, descendants of the founder of the college, who filled the office of college Visitor and appointed the Master. Until the college statutes were revised in the 1860s the Master enjoyed greater power than was usual in the head of a college, and by the terms of Pepys's will had a special authority over the Pepys Library. The College owned it, but the Master alone had custody of it. All these circumstances proved particularly fortunate in 1818. It is extremely unlikely that the college Fellows would have ventured to take any initiative in publishing a literary manuscript. The Master and his Neville uncles, on the other hand, all amateurs of literature and history, had contacts with the literary and publishing world of London. It was in effect they, not the college, who decided on publication and saw the project through. Which member of the family first promoted the idea we do not know, but within three or four months of the appearance of the Evelyn in April 1818 a sample volume of the Pepys was in London in the hands of Thomas Grenville, uncle of the Master and the bibliophile of the family. (It was his collection of books and pamphlets which was eventually bequeathed to the British Museum to form the Grenville Library.) He was, no doubt, familiar with the Pepys Library – his nephew had been Master of the College for the past five years – and it is likely enough that it was he who now suggested publication. As it happened, his brother Lord Grenville (Foreign Secretary under the Younger Pitt) had some knowledge of shorthand. Thomas therefore took the diary volume to William at his country house in Buckinghamshire, and on 18 August 1818 William was able to report to the Master that transcription was possible, and that if published the Pepys would form a 'delightful accompaniment' to the Evelyn. The Master then took charge of the project and commissioned an undergraduate to do the transcribing. Not an undergraduate of Magdalene – for Magdalene had only twenty-six all told and most of them were fellow-commoners of the sort that was to give Magdalene the reputation of being a riding not a reading college – but one John Smith of St John's, who had come up to the University encumbered with a wife and child, and was glad of the chance to earn the two hundred pounds which the Nevilles gave him for the work. He was provided with a key to the shorthand worked out by Lord Grenville and set to work in April 1819. He completed his task in three years, and despite the difficulties of the manuscript and the inadequacies of Grenville's key, he made a remarkably good attempt at a rendering. It would no doubt have been better had he been told that the Pepys Library contained the manual from which Pepys had himself learned the shorthand: Shelton's *Tutor to Tachygraphy* (1642). But Pepys never names the system, and at that time no one had identified it. It had been assumed that the Master would edit the work, but he was too busy and he handed over the task to his elder brother Richard Neville, who succeeded to the family title as Lord Braybrooke in 1825.

Braybrooke had an interest in history, though, as he later said, he preferred managing his estates and sitting on the Bench to working in his study. But he undertook this unexpected task as a family duty. He later published two other books — a history of the family home at Audley End and an edition of some family letters — again in the same cause. In his first edition of Pepys he reduced the text to one-quarter of its original size. As someone has rather unfairly remarked, 'it was the most severe operation on Pepys since his bladder stones were removed in 1658'. But the sheer length of the diary — about a million-and-a-quarter words — made drastic reduction necessary if it were to be published at all, especially since the plan (as with the Evelyn) included a selection of the diarist's correspondence. More-over, some of the omitted passages were considered (quite rightly) to be unprintable on legal grounds because of their indelicacy; others — much more numerous and lengthy and mostly about Pepys's work at the Navy Office — were omitted on the less convincing ground that Braybrooke thought the reader would find them 'tedious'.

Braybrooke's worst fault was not that he omitted so much, but that he inserted words and phrases of his own to bridge the gaps, without giving notice. His commentary, while it was not ambitious, was not greatly, if at all, inferior to that of William Bray, the con-temporary editor of Evelyn. Not surprisingly, his two volumes (pub-lished by Henry Colburn, who had brought out the Evelyn) were greeted with delight by the reviewers. He later brought out two other cheaper editions — in 1848–49 and in 1854 — which, although they sold in great numbers, were given a cooler welcome by the critics. In each of them he printed progressively more of Pepys's text and more footnotes, but his textual additions were slight and fell short of expectation, and his new footnotes were nothing more than random contributions made by assistants and correspondents. When he died in 1858 his reputation as an editor stood low.

It was not long before a new edition was projected. In 1864 George Bell and Son acquired the publication rights and soon made a tenta-tive agreement with a prospective editor. He was Rawson Lumby, the chaplain of Magdalene and an old boy of Leeds Grammar School. Lumby was an impressive, not to say a frightening man — a polymath who knew most European languages ancient and modern, and short-hand into the bargain, and a physical giant, over six feet tall and forty inches round the middle — all solid muscle — who could bend pokers with his bare hands. One of his Cambridge colleagues remarked of him that he was 'omnipotent and omniscient, but (thank Heaven) not omnipresent'. Later, after a spell at Leeds as Vice-Principal of the Theological College, he returned to Cambridge and became in 1879 Professor of Divinity, to be greeted by the verse: 'I heard the voice of Lumby say/I know six hundred creeds/I don't believe in one of them/We never did at Leeds.'

In 1868 his proposal to transcribe and publish Pepys afresh broke down against the resistance of Latimer Neville, Master of Magdalene and Braybrooke's son, who refused Lumby's request to work on the manuscript. But soon afterwards permission was granted to a senior Fellow of the College, who came to the task more by accident than design. He was the Rev. Mynors Bright, who had been forced to retire early from his college duties through illness, and decided to enliven the tedium of an invalid's life by making a new transcription of the Pepys. He published it with Bickers and Son in six volumes between 1875 and 1879, and included twice as much as Braybrooke had printed in his last edition. Bright was the first editor to learn the shorthand, and to disclose the fact — known to Lumby but unknown to both Smith and Braybrooke — that Pepys had used Shelton's system. But his text was more inaccurate than that of Smith and, since he was confined to an invalid's sofa, he was unable to add much commentary. The reviewers were hostile; his venture was a commercial failure, only one thousand copies being printed. He died shortly afterwards in 1883, leaving his manuscripts to Magdalene with the request that if any use were made of them for another edition, it should be published by Bells.

Bells opened negotiations with the college two years later in 1885, and in the '90s a new edition was produced which has stood to our own days as the standard edition. The editor was Henry Benjamin Wheatley, an accomplished London antiquarian, who had already declared his interest in Pepys by compiling the index to Bright's volumes and publishing a sort of commentary on the diary in 1880 as *Samuel Pepys and the World he Lived In*. Wheatley was a remarkable self-taught scholar — one of the same type and generation as Murray of the Oxford English Dictionary — and had that fresh and confident energy that is so often characteristic of the self-taught. He wrote a shelf-full of books on bibliographical, literary, and topographical subjects, and was a genial and popular member of the world of London bookmen, a founder of the Index Society (with which Dr Fitch himself has been for so long associated) and of other similar bodies, besides being an active member of half-a-dozen more. He brought out the ten volumes of his Pepys between 1893 and 1899, without ceasing to work on other tasks.

He made no transcription of his own, but used Bright's (whch was fuller in the manuscript version than in the printed version) and here and there a few passages from Smith's. The mistakes made by both — and they were many — he was unable to correct, having no knowledge of the shorthand and very little opportunity to study the original diary in Cambridge. But he was the first editor to omit the selections from Pepys's correspondence, and thus found room for about nine-tenths of the text. With commendable courage he included all the so-called 'tedious' passages and all but about ninety of the indelicate ones. These last were transcribed for him by Hugh Callendar, of Trinity College, a physicist with an interest in s .nography. Wheatley's courage reflects credit on both him and his publisher. His commentary was much the most extensive so far attempted but, like those of his predecessors, lacked consistency and method. Occasionally it was slight, and even irrelevant.

It is significant that none of these nineteenth-century editors, not even Wheatley, the most thorough of them, attempted to describe the diary manuscript or their methods of dealing with it. Nor did they attempt to assess its importance. They did not think of their function in these terms at all. They were interested in the man, not the document. Their introductions were biographical essays and nothing more. This was of course a policy, whatever its shortcomings, that suited the tastes of the reading public.

The Wheatley sold well, especially in the three-volume, thin-paper edition and in shorter versions, but eventually the need for a new edition made itself felt, and Bells made plans to replace it. The work was entrusted to Francis Turner, the Pepys Librarian at Magdalene, but although he made some progress it became clear that he would need help. I was asked to help him, and came to the conclusion that a new start had to be made. I was allowed to take charge and make my own plans: Mr Turner, by that time about to retire from his college posts, retired also from the editorship. My first step was to find someone who would take on the transcription. I had learned the shorthand, but was not fluent in it and had no expert knowledge of the forms of the language in seventeenth-century England. There was only one man who filled the bill, and fortunately he was delighted to do it. He was Will Matthews, a professor of English at the University of California at Los Angeles, who in 1935 in the *Journal of English and Germanic Philology* had published a study of the Shelton shorthand and, in 1950, had brought out a descriptive bibliography of British diaries. Other subjects on which he had published ranged from the medieval language and literature of England to modern Cockney (and the latter proved not without relevance to a study of Pepys's pronunciation). Matthews arranged to spend two sabbatical leaves in England, beginning in 1961, and during these transcribed the manuscript afresh. He worked rapidly, and handed over to me, in instalments, a vast and beautiful typescript. I read it slowly, checking it against the manuscript wherever points struck either of us as uncertain, and on the look-out in particular for doubtful readings that could best be cleared up by a historian, such as names of persons and places, or technical terms in naval administration. Matthews later rechecked the entire typescript against the original with the help of his wife. The work of transcription was substantially his and it is to him that we owe the new text. It was a great blow when he died in 1976, but fortunately he had by that time completed virtually all his share of the work. He had originally been interested in Pepys because Pepys wrote a phonetic shorthand, and his 1938 article was the first systematic attempt to bring the evidence of shorthand to bear on the problem of how the language was spoken in south-east England in the seventeenth century. He now produced a text of the diary, in which the (editorial) longhand spelling – used wherever Pepys could be shown to have employed the same longhand forms himself – reflects Pepys's pronunciation. He also provided textual footnotes giving alternative readings where the manuscript was unclear, and carrying information about Pepys's method of composition – about, for instance, the alterations and additions that he made as he wrote.

We cannot claim that what we have printed is exactly what Pepys would have written had he composed the diary in longhand, for, apart from any mistakes of our own, his spelling varied (as most people's did), and the abbreviated forms of the shorthand which he often used do not always give enough information about what variant he had in mind. In fact we had to spell in modern style wherever we had no guide from the sounds represented by the shorthand and no knowledge of Pepys's normal orthography. His capitalisation of the longhand (often very odd) was reproduced exactly, and so was his paragraphing. His punctuation was almost non-existent; we had to provide it. Giving due notice (by footnotes or square brackets), we corrected obvious errors — the commonest being his omission of words at line-endings where his mind was apt to jump ahead of his pen. Others were small slips such as 'Mr' for 'Mrs', 'Lord Chancellor' for 'Lord Chamberlain' and so on. But we did not attempt to normalise his idiosyncratic English (as the nineteenth-century editors did), nor did we set ourselves up in judgement on him by removing or bowdlerising the indelicate passages. We were lucky in that the Obscene Publications Act of 1959 had made the way clear to publish the diary in its entirety, by giving legal protection against prosecution to works of literary or historical merit. The indelicate passages now appeared for the first time as Pepys wrote them. Where they were amorous, they were written in a comical macaronic mixture of English, French and Spanish for the most part. Edward Wilson, Professor of Spanish at Cambridge, helped us to get the Spanish right — the rest presented no difficulties, linguistic or otherwise.

Matthews and I shared an introduction, of which a short biography by me was the least important section, and in which we concentrated on describing the manuscript, its history, its treatment by previous editors, and our own methods. It ended with essays on the literary interest and historical value of the diary — subjects not previously broached by the editors of Pepys or by anybody else. Historians have not tackled the subject — they have been content to plunder the diary for quotations, rather than study it. Nor have literary critics: they are not drawn to the study of diaries. Diaries are hardly an art-form like novels, and the study of any one of them does not reveal anything about diaries in general. Each diarist writes (as Pepys did) by his own lights.

As for the explanatory notes, responsibility was divided between myself and a number of contributors and advisers. These were experts in the subjects I could not pretend to know well enough — that is, the drama, London topography, music, the fine arts and the weather. What remained for me to do was still enough to keep my leisure innocently filled for over twenty years. I had no lack of source materials. Pepys himself had left me plenty. In the Pepys Library there are scores of his naval papers of the diary period — among them a shorthand diary of office matters, his 'Navy White Book', in which he related sometimes the same events as those recorded in the personal diary, but with interesting variations of detail — and from a later period his 'Navall Minutes', a commonplace book in which his more mature reflections are entered. And as one would expect, the Library, though much changed after 1669 when the diary ended, contains a number of the books mentioned in it. Often enough when working there I could walk a few paces from my desk to pick out from the shelf the very copy Pepys refers to — the number of shelf-marks would settle the question of whether it was the same copy or one acquired later (for he was fond of replacing his books). Almost the only memorably difficult book to find in the Library, I think, was a book of tales which Pepys refers to by the title of the second tale, which does not appear on the title-page.

Much of his personal correspondence is in the Bodleian Library, where there are some eighty volumes of his letters and papers. An admirable guide to them, in the form of a list and index, was issued by the Bodleian in 1862 and 1878. Some of the letters have been published — by R. G. Howarth in 1933; others by Helen Heath in 1955 as *The Family Letters of Samuel Pepys*. Four of Pepys's own letter-books were passed down through the family of his sister Paulina to her descendants, the Pepys Cockerells. These are still in private hands (though not those of the Pepys Cockerells), and are difficult of access, but almost all were printed by Dr J. R. Tanner in three volumes in 1926 and 1929.

The most voluminous of Pepys's manuscripts for the diary period are his Navy Board papers in the Public Record Office and elsewhere. His gift for keeping full, exact, and beautifully organised records was one of the secrets of his great success as a civil servant. Many of them now serve the cause of historical research as efficiently as once they served their original purpose. A volume of Pepys's copies of his out-letters (or the more important of them) has found its way (via the Pepys Cockerells) to the National Maritime Museum. The in-letters and other papers are in the Public Record Office and (by a piece of great good fortune for Pepys's editor) have been listed, summarised and indexed in the *Calendars of State Papers, Domestic*. These large fat volumes have been my El Dorado, my mines of Peru.

The Public Record Office also has other papers of interest for my purpose: the records of the Privy Council and the Secretaries of State and those of the national Treasury and of the Navy Treasury, both of which have rich seams of Pepysian material, since the Navy Board was the biggest spender of government departments. The ledgers of the Navy Treasury were of particular value. These were drawn up each quarter and list, for each of the royal dockyards, the officers and their clerks, with their salaries and allowances; and, under separate headings, the supplies they bought – 'Ironwork', 'Deals', 'Tar', and so on. They tell us much about Pepys's office life and occasionally something about his home life, since he lived in lodgings maintained at government expense. I went off to the Public Record Office whenever, as it were, the workmen arrived in Pepys's house to lay a new floor or to redecorate the exterior, to see what I could find out. Unfortunately, the bills and the ledgers give totals for the whole of the Office building without differentiating between the lodgings. But at any rate I had the satisfaction of learning that the workmen used three coats of oil-bound paint and that there were one hundred and eighty-one windows in the building and one hundred and sixty-eight yards of paling round it. When the Navy Board had a gallery built for their use in their parish church, St Olave's, Hart St (there were three rows of seats and predictable disputes about the order of seating among the officials and their womenfolk), I was confident I should easily enough find the ledger's record of the payment to the dockyard workmen who were employed to build it. But for a while it eluded my search. I eventually found it in the section entitled 'Extra Service on the Seas'. But accountancy is a strange art. And the art has its reasons that reason cannot tell.

Clearly if Pepys had not been a public servant his diary would have been much more difficult to edit. And equally, if he had lived elsewhere than in London. But the topography of Pepys's London is established in some detail by contemporary maps and views, such as those by Hollar, some of them products of the Great Fire, and by late seventeenth-century guide books, such as Delaune's *Angliae Metropolis*, as well as by Strype's *Stow* and more modern works. As a result, it is not difficult for the editor to find his way round most of the streets and alleys of Pepys's London. And thanks to the recent work of Professor Downes and others it is even possible to follow Pepys's movements as he walks in the galleries of Whitehall Palace, that royal rabbit warren which was the centre of his world.

The same problems arose in identifying the three thousand or so persons whom Pepys mentions. Many can be traced in the standard biographical reference books and printed genealogies. Others can be found in the records of national taxation – and for the diary period we have the hearth-tax and two poll-taxes whose records give not only the names and parishes of individuals, but also information about the sizes of their houses and households. A large proportion of Pepys's business acquaintances were navy contractors and turn up in the archives of the Navy Office. Others may be traced in the records of the City livery companies. But if these and similar sources fail, the editor's task is made much less difficult by the fact that so many of Pepys's characters were Londoners by birth or residence and can, with luck, be tracked down in parish records — registers, church-wardens' accounts, and ratebooks — which, almost without exception, are conveniently gathered in three repositories: the Guildhall Library, Westminster City Library and the Record Office of the former GLC. By an extra piece of good luck, many of the registers have been printed and indexed by the Harleian and Index Societies. There are also alphabetical guides to the registers — the most remarkable being the enormous name index published on microfiches by the Mormons, who need to know the names of their ancestors. Latter-Day sinners like myself have reason to be grateful for their pains.

With all these aids it has been possible to identify most of the characters, however obscure. Those who gave me the greatest diffi-culty, and often defeated me, were: junior clerks in government departments paid by their superiors and not by the state; officers in the merchant navy; foreigners who did not become denizens or naturalised subjects; Roman Catholic priests, and those married women whose maiden names could not be discovered.

If it was fortunate that Pepys was a Londoner, it was also fortunate that I too was a Londoner when doing most of my research, for the editor of Pepys has to tackle many subjects and needs the resources of the great libraries and archives of the capital. Splendid institutions, and almost without exception splendidly served by their staffs. The only exception I found — and I can be frank for things have now changed — was at Somerset House, where were kept the contempor-ary registers of the wills proved in the diocese of Canterbury — essential tools for biographical work. The registers are large and repulsive volumes — the heaviest and dirtiest books I ever came across. These it was the duty of the officials to carry from the stacks to the readers' desks. At one end of the reading room was an official (clerical grade) to whom one handed one's application slip (he was reading the *Daily Telegraph*); at the other end was an official (messen-ger grade) who fetched the volumes. (He was reading the *Daily Mirror*.) And it was the aim of each to go on reading his paper rather than get my volumes out. But, as I say, all that has now changed.

The wills for my period are now kept in the Public Record Office, available on microfilm, and the officers in charge at Somerset House, presumably, are left undisturbed with their newspapers.

I found that my work also took me on trips out of London for visits to museums and record offices and occasionally to country houses to look at family documents. My visits were not always attended with success. In Bristol I searched in vain for traces of the family of the unfortunate Deb Willet; in Deptford and its environs I failed to find out anything about the wife of the complaisant ship's carpenter William Bagwell. But women, as I say, can be very difficult, and the hunt was the fun. Sometimes, as in the course of my researches I strolled with the peacocks on the terrace of a country house, or sat before a plate of whitebait in a Greenwich pub, I was tempted to feel that it would not matter whether the new edition of Pepys's diary saw the light of day or not. Enough to have had a hunt through unexplored manuscripts, and an outing in the bargain.

In deploying my commentary and that of my colleagues within the pages of the edition, I had to think first and foremost of the reader's convenience. All the notes on scribal aspects of the manuscript — alternative readings and so on — had to appear on the page immediately under the printed text. So did amplifications, verifications and corrections. But there was, in addition, a great deal of relevant information which the reader does not need to have under his eye as he reads, and which can be tucked away elsewhere in appendixes of various sorts. Words are glossed in this way (though I put asterisks by them in the text if they look easy but are really difficult — i.e. if they have changed their meaning). As for places, when they are mentioned they have a footnote only if Pepys's reference to them is obscure or calls for comment for some other reason. At 22 January 1660, there is a clear case of obscurity (if the phrase is allowable) when Pepys states that he went to 'Heaven'. A footnote had to be added to explain that it was a tavern. (When Heaven recurs in the text some weeks later, the temptation was almost irresistible to write simply: 'For Heaven, see above'.)

Persons are often roughly identified in the text by Pepys's own words, as 'Commissioner Pett' or 'Aunt Fenner' and so on. That is enough for most readers, and a fuller account can be given elsewhere. But they require footnotes if the reference is obscure — Pepys not infrequently uses a personal pronoun without relating it clearly to a specific person, or he spells a name strangely, or refers to a man by the title of his office, or fails to distinguish between several Thomases. Persons also call for footnotes when their identity has to be known by the reader if he is to understand the text properly. Dr Pearse's tales about the ladies of the court are only appreciated if the reader is told at the foot of the page that he was a court surgeon. The identity of the people who give Pepys his political news, in particular, has to be made clear on the page if Pepys himself does not do so. His information may be mere gossip, or it may be — and usually is — hard news, as retailed by a Privy Council clerk or the like. And if Pepys does not identify his source, the editor should.

For the most part, the footnotes were designed to deal with the running narrative. They are about situations and events. When on 22 December 1660 Pepys dines as a guest of Captain Teddeman at the Sun tavern on Fish St Hill, the note does not give thumb-nail biographies of the other guests he names, but simply points out that all were concerned one way or another with the ransoming of English captives taken by Barbary corsairs. Again, when on 1 September 1664 Pepys reports that at dinner he had 'a great cake Moorcock lately sent us', the footnote does not deal in general terms with Moorcock or the habit of giving cakes as presents, but states (what Pepys does not state there or elsewhere) that on that same day, Moorcock, who was a timber merchant, had sent to the Navy Board a tender for the supply of elm.

I am both a believer in footnotes and a sceptic about them, and I confess that I have come to have two literary models in mind when composing them — Beachcomber's Prodnose and P. G. Wodehouse's Jeeves. The writer of notes should avoid being Prodnose — always popping up with unwanted interjections, and should model himself on Jeeves — remaining discreetly out of sight in the pantry, but ready to shimmer in when needed.

I spoke a few moments ago of the material tucked away for reference. Some of it was hived off into a List of Persons and a Select Glossary which appeared at the end of each volume of text, so that every volume was for most purposes self-sufficient. But most of it was hived off into a supplementary volume entitled the *Companion*, in which articles of several sorts and sizes were combined in a single alphabetical series. There, as in the other volumes, I called in help from experts, among them my Magdalene colleague Richard Luckett, who has contributed not only a remarkable article on Music, but also the article on Language and the Large Glossary of Words which

Professor Matthews had not lived to write. I also persuaded a New York psychoanalyst to write on Pepys's psyche. He treated the revelations of the diary as though they were confessions made on the couch, and found himself, as he told me, dealing with the first healthy man he has ever found there.

The eleventh and final volume of the edition is the Index, on which I worked for about four years, with my wife, poor wretch. This was my first attempt at a big index — I suspect nobody survives to do more than one anyway. Indexes combine the pleasures of a jig-saw puzzle with those of a Victorian paper game. You play around with hundreds of page-references so that they fit into a design, and you have to find the appropriate word or phrase to indicate the subject of the references. I began by reading manuals on the subject, and then went on to read other people's indexes. Some, like Dr de Beer's index to his Evelyn, give you a model to follow, though you know you will never do it half as well. Others are examples of how not to do it, especially if they consist of headings followed by nothing but page-numbers. Some again can be very revealing. Those of you who have, for instance, read and enjoyed the writings of Hugh Trevor-Roper, may have missed reading his indexes, where you will find sometimes even more to read and enjoy. He is free with his opinions in the books themselves, but here and there in the indexes he really lets fly. For example in his index to his book of essays *Renaissance, Reformation and Social Change,* you will find his views on several subjects: on Saints ('Aquinas, St Thomas: advantages of ignoring him'); on Scotsmen ('Irvine of Drum, Sir Alexander: a sensible Scotsman'); and on his fellow historians ('Hill, Christopher: highly praised, p. 243; less highly, p. 194').

I didn't achieve these effects in the index to Pepys, but I enjoyed doing it. It meant, for one thing, listening to the diary being read aloud. My wife read it while I, at the other side of the table, made notes (a rough draft of the notes having been made beforehand by a research assistant). I discovered — what I ought to have known before — that my ears read better than my eyes. We teach our eyes from early youth to read quickly, and therefore miss a lot. When we depend on our ears we drop to the pace of the spoken word, and catch details which have escaped our eyes. I found, for instance, that when my wife's voice told me (as she read) that Pepys's neigh-bour Sir Richard Ford, a merchant acting as a tax assessor, had put Pepys's rate rather higher than Pepys thought fair, I remembered her voice telling me a day or two before that Pepys had annoyed Sir Richard by condemning the hemp he had sold to the navy. Sir Richard may have been getting his own back.

One of the principles of the design of the Index was to gather as many references as possible into clusters — under general terms such as 'Food', 'Drink', 'Dress' and so on — so that the Index could enable the diary to serve as a book of reference. Another aim was to reduce to a minimum the uninformative references — those that had to be described as 'allusions' or 'miscellaneous'. One means of achieving this was the use of the category 'social' which I adopted from Dr de Beer's index to his Evelyn. It was even more valuable for Pepys's diary, with its much higher count of dinner parties and general hobnobbing. Thus the entry on Sir William Penn (which occupies six columns) has only two references under the heading 'alluded to' — only two extras or leg-byes as it were; for the rest, a run scored off every ball.

A further concern was to make sure that each reference was indexed in the right place. How, for instance, do you index Pepys's references to his health? Remedies are easy — you have only to list names: balsam, enemas, rabbits' feet, and so on. But diseases can be difficult: you have only Pepys's description of his symptoms to go on and you have to decide when he writes of 'taking cold' whether to index it under 'colds/coughs/sore throats', or under 'colic', or whether to leave it doubtful. Fortunately, for the entry on Health I was able to consult Dr Charles Newman of the Royal College of Physicians, who combines a scholar's knowledge of seventeenth-century medicine with modern clinical experience. Or again, when Pepys goes to the Exchequer, it is necessary to ask whether his visit relates to his work in the Navy Office or his work as Treasurer of the Tangier Commitee. I found that often this could not be settled, and the Index at these points leaves it doubtful.

Several people told me when I started work on the Index that I ought to use a computer. But it would have been extremely difficult (as well as expensive and time-consuming) to programme the machine. I doubt in fact if a computer can be used for indexing a text like Pepys, in which there are so many indirect, submerged and ambiguous references. To have determined who was meant by 'my Uncle' or by 'the Duke' or by unattached pronouns and so on, would have meant continually going back to the text. A computer print-out would have been awkward to handle, with its rows of figures in which the eye loses its way. Again, I was advised to have the index made for me by someone else — by an expert on indexes. But Pepys's diary can only be indexed from the inside — from a knowledge of its contents and their interconnections. I had already come to this conclusion when I read the opening sentence of the manual on indexing published by the Cambridge University Press. There the author, G. V. Carey, says in effect: 'Get someone else to write your book for you if you like — but be sure you write your own index.'

Well, I wrote the Index: but the important thing is that it was Pepys who wrote the book.

ROBERT SHACKLETON was for many years a Fellow and Tutor in
Modern Languages of Brasenose College, Oxford. A noted bibliophile
and academic administrator, he was Bodley's Librarian 1966–79, and
subsequently Marshal Foch Professor of French literature until his
death in 1986. He published extensively and wrote the authoritative
biography of Montesquieu. He held numerous doctorates (*honoris
causa*) and awards, was a leading member of the British Academy,
President of the International Society for Eighteenth-Century
Studies, Chevalier de la Légion d'Honneur (1982), and was appointed
CBE shortly before his death. As Lyell Reader in Bibliography at
Oxford he lectured on the bibliography of Montesquieu. His outstanding Montesquieu collection was bequeathed to the Bodleian
Library, but the greater part of the remainder of his fine library is
in the John Rylands University Library of Manchester.

Old books in the university library

ROBERT SHACKLETON

A well-nurtured library is, historically, an integral part of any country house, and to possess such a library was, for centuries, fashionable. The uncomprehending owner has long been a subject of mockery. Alexander Pope, in his *Epistle to Lord Burlington*, attacks under the name of Timon a victim not yet plausibly identified, whose study is particularly vulnerable:

> His Study! with what Authors is it stor'd?
> In Books, not Authors, curious is my Lord;
> To all their dated Backs he turns you round,
> Those Aldus printed, those Du Seuil has bound.
> Lo some are vellum, and the rest as good
> For all his Lordship knows, but they are Wood.
> For Locke or Milton 'tis in vain to look,
> These shelves admit not any modern book.

The modern equivalent of this unnamed Lord is the millionaire whose shelves contain railway timetables lavishly bound in red morocco.

Between such as these, and the genuine, informed collector, there is all the difference in the world. The collections of a Lord Crawford, a Henry Huntington, a Lord Brotherton, a Mary Hyde are themselves monuments of scholarship, and often enough find their final home in the public domain. The scholar's task is often immensely facilitated by their richness and by their unity of theme.

The really great rare-book collections in our University libraries have most frequently as their base the generosity of benefactors. The historic collections of the Bodleian have come to the Library sometimes by purchase, sometimes by copyright deposit, sometimes by donation; but of these three channels, the most prolific is undoubtedly that of donation, either during the donor's lifetime or, more frequently, by bequest. The illustrious names of Archbishop Laud, of Richard Rawlinson, of Francis Douce, stand on the Bodleian's marble tablet of benefactors. The value of their gifts to the Library can hardly be expressed in modern or monetary terms, nor can anyone today envisage the alienation of such treasures.

The fact that the great bulk of such material has come by gift does not exonerate those responsible for the Library from using the Library's own resources to add to its rare book resources, whether (to use well-worn phrases) they are filling gaps or building on strength. Thus, when I went to the Bodleian, I found we had a better-than-average collection of the essays of Montaigne crying out for improvement. When I left the Library, I am glad to say that we had an excellent collection of that author.

What should be the policy relating to old books, of those responsible for libraries which operate on a more modest scale than the Bodleian?

I remember hearing the Director of one of the richest American university libraries say, some twenty years ago, that he believed it to be his duty to eliminate books from his library and that de-acquisition was as important a task as acquisition. I am still puzzled by that assertion, which might be true of an undergraduate library but not of a major learned library. His reasoning was certainly not that of an important New York bookseller who told me that he thought every learned library ought to de-acquisition seven per cent of its stock each year and release it to the book trade. No! the state of the true learned library must be a state of regular but controlled expansion.

This obviously raises the question of definition. Not all university libraries are true learned libraries. This name can be given in the first place to the libraries of Oxford and Cambridge. The libraries of Manchester and Leeds are to be included; so also those of Edinburgh and Glasgow; some of those in London University; perhaps one or two more.

A particular problem is raised by the College libraries of Oxford and Cambridge, which are partly undergraduate libraries, partly small rare-book libraries. They have very restricted room for growth. Their librarians often aim at the exclusion of eighteenth-century sermons — a very elastic category.

I have myself bought from an Oxford bookseller various books recently eliminated from different College libraries: the first collective edition of the work of Nicholas-Antoine Boulanger, a minor, but most original French *philosophe* in whom I was particularly interested;

an immaculate copy of the second edition of Barthélemy's *Voyage du jeune Anacharsis en Grèce*; two editions of the English translation of Montesquieu's *De l'Esprit des lois*. These came from three different College libraries. Add the fact that I paid no more than three pounds for each of them, allow for the bookseller's profit and you see that the Colleges had a most meagre return for their sale.

Colleges are not now supposed to eliminate books from their collections without giving the Bodleian the opportunity of acquiring them. I hope, but am not confident, that this rule is always followed. One can hardly think, however, of books being sold from Christ Church Library, the Codrington Library of All Souls, or from Trinity College, Cambridge.

Indeed, some major learned libraries have eliminated books from their shelves. A Paris bookseller of high quality was once browsing among my own books. As he looked at one eighteenth-century book he turned to me with what they call an old-fashioned look. The book was the 1758 *Almanach royal*. It bore an eighteenth-century armorial binding, and the arms were those of the King of France, in the form which the Royal Library (the precursor of the Bibliothèque Nationale) used for its books. He opened the volume and saw a shelfmark as used in the past by the Bibliothèque du roi. I then urged him to turn to the title page, where he saw the mark of a Jesuit College at Heiligenstadt, near Göttingen, with the date 1764. It is true that I bought the book in the 1950s from the catalogue of a Leipzig bookseller.

Well-known is the story of the Bodleian copy of the first folio edition of Shakespeare. When the second folio appeared the first folio was deemed superseded, and was eliminated from the Library. It was seen again in 1905 when an undergraduate brought it into the Library for advice about its binding; it was identified by a binder's mark and re-acquisitioned by purchase. Truly one can say, 'Habent sua fata libelli'.

It is not enough, however, to assert the importance of old books. The assertion must be supported by reasoning. There is a difference between the buying of old books, and their retention when they are already possessed. There are few libraries which could contemplate the purchase of the Gutenberg or 42-line Bible, if ever it became available. A few years ago one copy was in the market. It was sold to a New York dealer by a private collector, whose insurer had declined to continue insuring it as long as he kept it in his house. He decided that the pleasure of ownership would be much diminished if the book had to be locked up in his bank. Accordingly he sold it to Mr Kraus, leaving only one copy in the hands of a private person. The price I cannot specify, but it must have been high, since it was placed on offer for two and a half million dollars. Eventually it was sold – the purchaser being the University of Texas. This surprised me, since the Texas Library is not a noted collector of printed books, as opposed to manuscripts. I expressed my surprise to a professor at Texas, who replied, 'You forget that we are talking about the oldest edition of the Bible'.

Only the greatest libraries could afford *not* to sell the Gutenberg Bible. If the Bodleian were to sell its copy, which is particularly fine, its reputation would suffer a permanent decline. A library strong in incunabula, often visited by scholars specialising in the fifteenth century, needs its 42-line Bible. A small college library of general interest, which happened to possess this work, would find its fortunes transformed if it could invest more than a million pounds and spend the interest. But any university library should possess a few incunabula, so that its students might see how books were produced in the fifteenth century, how well the paper and the type have survived for five hundred years, and compare them with the products of today, which can scarcely look forward to a century of life.

I am concerned mainly, however, with books of the sixteenth-, seventeenth- and eighteenth centuries. Let us say first that in those centuries there were produced works of reference which have not been superseded. The *Grand Dictionnaire historique* of Moreri, first published in 1673, and frequently republished and expanded until 1759, is still a most valuable work of reference. I myself possess the edition of 1698 (in four folio volumes) and that of 1740 (in eight volumes), and for my own researches I find them invaluable. The Bodleian keeps the 1759 edition on open shelves. This work gives more historical, geographical, and genealogical information in less space than any other work I know. The Benedictine monks of St Maur produced in the eighteenth century *L'Art de vérifier les dates*, likewise a precious instrument for chronological information. Linguistic dictionaries teach us much about historical linguistics, and particularly the history of semantics. Old maps have a clear value. One understands better the Grand Tour of the eighteenth- and early-nineteenth centuries, if one can use the actual maps which the travellers used, and the guide books which accompanied them.

I have mentioned the French *Almanachs royaux* which began

under Louis XIV and continued to the Second Empire. They provide the best means of ascertaining office-holders in Paris and in the provinces. In England, let us note the invaluable *Annual Register* and the *Gentleman's Magazine*. In Italy, the *Storia dell'Anno* appeared annually from 1742 to 1806 and gave a detailed account of events in each country for the year in question.

It might be thought that it was unnecessary to acquire or to keep the original editions of works of which good, modern, critical editions existed. Even here we must be careful. Few works have been truly edited with full rigour. Even the *Lettres Philosophiques* of Voltaire, Lanson's critical edition of which is a model of editing, requires for its full comprehension, reference to the early texts. Historical bibliography or *la bibliographie matérielle* was a closed book to Lanson.

And not to Lanson alone. Indeed, the study of historical bibliography is a recent phenomenon whose development has been strong in Leeds, thanks to Professor John Horden. The detailed study of printing is as much a prerequisite for the reliable establishment of the critical text of a work subsequent to the fifteenth century, as the study of paleography is for the mediaeval work.

Let me give an example from the first edition of Alexander Pope's *Essay on Man*. As you will know, this poem consists of four epistles which were originally published separately. The first collective edition, of 1734, was issued in three forms – in quarto, in small folio, and in large folio. Of the large folio three copies only are known, of which two are in American libraries, while one, by a happy chance, belongs to me. In the printing of my copy, a serious mistake was made on p. 44. What should have read

> . . . they began
> Whom they rever'd as God, to mourn as Man.

The word 'rever'd' was misprinted as 'revers'd'. Clearly so gross an error had to be corrected at whatever cost. A new leaf was printed and glued into the volume. This is what we call the cancellans. The original leaf, the cancellandum, by an error in my copy, was not removed, so that pp. 43–44 are repeated. The signatures, however, are odd. The cancellandum was [K2], though not actually carrying a signature. The cancellans, which ought to be similarly [K2], carries the signature L.

How are we to explain this? My suggestion is that when sheet K was set, it was proofed without the detection of the error. The sheet was then printed and the type distributed. The error was detected at this stage, it was decided to print a cancel at once, and it was printed immediately on sheet L. This is my hypothesis which I shall test against the two other copies on my next visit to America. Two copies of the small folio are known, and both are in Bodley. One of them exactly resembles mine; in the other the cancellandum has been removed, and L1 is lacking. This is a very intricate problem. There exists a critical edition of the *Essay on Man*, by Maynard Mack. It is an excellent edition so far as the ideas and sources of the poem are concerned, but the cancels are not discussed at all.

Another example of the necessity of the bibliographical approach is Voltaire's *Candide*. First published in 1759, many editions were published in that year. Mr Giles Barber has identified seventeen in all, fifteen of which are in the Taylor Institution at Oxford, one at Yverdon, and one in my own collection. The first edition is believed to have been published by Cramer at Geneva. How are we to identify that edition among the collection? The researches of my late colleague Richard Sayce, embodied in an article in *The Library*, make it easier than it would otherwise have been to approach this problem. What Sayce did was to examine a large number of collections of books published in Western Europe under the *ancien régime* and to establish the typographical conventions of the different countries: the presence or absence of catchwords, the nature and occurrence of the signatures, the form of the pagination and of the date. To these we can add the press figures – whose presence is indicative of an English origin.

These conventions give most useful indications of the origin of a book; but they are not always decisive, because printers were well aware of the conventions of other nations, and when a French book was being printed with a Dutch imprint they were perfectly capable of following Dutch printing conventions to add to the plausibility of the imprint.

A further means of identifying the origin of a book can sometimes be afforded by the study of the *fleurons* or printers ornaments. This technique has not yet been carried to its most useful point, and the individual researcher must examine the typographical specimen sheets issued by different printers. The late Ira Wade, of Princeton, initiated this study in relation to *Candide*. I was once showing him a copy of the *Traité des trois imposteurs.* He asked to look at the title page upside down. I then saw an ornament of flowers and bugles thought to be used by Cramer. The study has been taken further at the Taylor Institution, where an extensive file of ornaments has been established. This will perhaps be published by the Voltaire Foundation. It would be most useful if such a file could be started at the Brotherton Collection.

I should like now to examine further the utility of these methods by examining the case of Montesquieu, whose bibliography I am now seeking to establish. Let us look first at the *Lettres persanes*, the original edition of which appeared in 1721 with the imprint 'Cologne, chez Pierre Marteau'. Anyone with a reasonable knowledge of the history of book production in the period knows that this is a false imprint. The name 'Pierre Marteau' appears on a very large number of books of the late seventeenth- and the early eighteenth century. Sometimes it appears in Latin, 'Petrus de Martellis'; sometimes in Italian, 'Pietro Martelli'; sometimes in German, 'Peter Hammer'. His books are usually of small format. But the man is non-existent. The use of his name was a well-understood convention, which meant 'This book is unusual and independent, and had better not be submitted for approval by the ordinary channels'.

Where did the *Lettres persanes* appear? We know from the Abbé Guasco, a later friend of Montesquieu, that a secretary was sent to Amsterdam to arrange the publication. We know also that Montesquieu's historical work on the *Grandeur et décadence des Romains* was published at Amsterdam by Jacques Desbordes. A careful examination of the two works reveals that they issued from the same printing-house. We are then justified in attributing the first edition of the *Lettres persanes* to Jacques Desbordes. This does not apply, however, to all editions of the *Lettres persanes* with the same Cologne imprint. This imprint was attached by the publisher to the *Lettres persanes*, and was used on later editions when they were in reality published by other Amsterdam printers, by Paris printers, by Rouen printers, at Lausanne, at Copenhagen, or at London.

The publication of *De l'Esprit des lois* was not less complicated. The first edition, unsuitable for normal publication in Paris, appeared at Geneva with a truthful imprint 'A Genève, chez Barrillot et fils'. This was followed by a whole host of editions, issued at Paris, at London, at Amsterdam, with the same Geneva imprint. Not all these were pirated editions, but one pirate, which sought closely to imitate the first editions, made the bibliographer's task easier by mis-spelling the printer's name as 'Barillot'.

When we come to editions of the complete work published first in 1758 when Montesquieu was dead, we find the imprint, unconvincing at first, 'Amsterdam et Leipzig, Arkstée et Merkus'. These two gentlemen did exist; they were half-brothers and lived in Amsterdam, with an office in Leipzig for the fairs. The edition was in fact, as we know from external evidence, published in Paris. Was any payment made to Arkstée et Merkus for the use of their name? Were they perhaps allowed to publish themselves an edition in small format if they left the quarto edition to the Paris publisher? We know that in other cases similar arrangements were made, though no international protection of copyright existed in the eighteenth century.

I should like to bring the discussion back to the university library. I think it has become clear first, that in order to study a text thoroughly and to learn all that it can tell us, we must not content ourselves with modern editions or even with facsimile reprints, but must go to the original texts; and secondly, that it is a desirable policy for the library to acquire copies of as many editions as possible.

This policy has been pursued by the Bodleian Library, most notably in the case of John Locke. Owing to the munificence of benefactors, the Bodleian has the great bulk of the surviving manuscripts of Locke, including his journals, and a large part of his own library, which we have been able to arrange on the shelves in the actual order in which Locke had placed them. It was decided, some twenty years ago, to try to acquire all editions of Locke, ancient or modern, in English or in translation. This is an excellent policy and enables us to have an admirable view of the influence and range of England's greatest philosopher.

We should not even despise the acquisition of duplicates, provided that they are not very expensive. The Folger Shakespeare Library of Washington has acquired very many copies of the rare folio and quarto editions of Shakespeare, though I doubt whether my proviso about price applied here. In my more modest collecting of Montesquieu I have not eschewed duplicates, and have often found in the end that they were not true duplicates. Let me cite the case of the *Lettres familières,* which is the first edition of Montesquieu's correspondence. The original edition of this work was published in Florence in 1767. I acquired my copy of it in Naples, some forty years ago, for one hundred and fifty lire. Three years ago I found another copy, in Florence, for fifty thousand lire, a somewhat larger sum but not unreasonable. I decided to acquire it. On my return to Oxford, I compared the two and found that the title pages differed, in that the second copy misspelt the name of Montesquieu, omitting the first 'u'. Since normally an error precedes the correct form, it appeared that the second form was the true first edition, and had been corrected by a variant title leaf.

I must apologise for talking so much about my own research and my own collection, but it is better to be well acquainted with one's evidence. I would make a suggestion about terminology which should apply to a library like the Leeds University Library. We should not talk of old books as rare books or as collectors' pieces or as antiquarian books. We should talk of them as research material. The study of books is in many respects a new discipline; at least it is a discipline with new methods. These new methods have been taught in Anglo-Saxon countries, by R. B. McKerrow, by Fredson Bowers, by William Todd, by Philip Gaskell, and by Donald McKenzie. They are being taught now, perhaps even on a wider scale, in France, by Henri-Jean Martin and his disciples. His earlier studies of the relationship between government and book production are now being consolidated into his splendid four-volume *Histoire de l'édition française*. The relationship between bibliography and social history has been emphasised by Robert Darnton at Princeton. Indeed, bibliography belongs to social history, to technical history, and to intellectual history, and in this dominant position is a proper and necessary subject for study in a university. Books, and particularly old books, are its raw material and as such have a proper and necessary place in the university.

D. F. McKENZIE, Professor of Bibliography and Textual Criticism
and Fellow of Pembroke College, Oxford, is a New Zealander who,
for many years, was Professor of English Language and Literature,
Victoria University, Wellington. Among his main publications are
Stationers' Company Apprentices, 1605–1800 (3 vols, 1961–78); *The
Cambridge University Press, 1696–1712* (2 vols, 1966); *Oral Culture,
Literacy and Print in Early New Zealand* (1985); *Bibliography and
the Sociology of Texts* (1986). He was Sandars Reader in Bibliography
at Cambridge in 1976, he delivered the inaugual series of Panizzi
Lectures for the British Library in 1985, and was Lyell Reader in
Bibliography at Oxford in 1988. Professor McKenzie was President of
the Bibliographical Society, 1982–83 (Gold Medal, 1990), and is a
Fellow of the British Academy.

The London book trade in 1644

D. F. McKENZIE

I was intrigued to note at a recent seminar that a minor typing error in the programme had transformed the distinguished Institute of Bibliography and Textual Criticism here at Leeds into one of Bibliography and Textual 'Cohesion'. And of course, like many mis-readings, it is not quite so absurd as one might think. For a decade in which the key critical term has been 'deconstruction', it might indeed be time to bring things together, to build a new synthesis, and to proclaim as our motto, like Adam Overdo at the end of Jonson's *Bartholomew Fair*, '*Ad correctionem, non ad destructionem; ad aedificandum, non ad diruendum*'.

If the challenge is to create a new synthesis, to trace relationships between the disciplines, to complement the deficiencies of one by the strengths of another, then it happens to be a challenge which bibliography is exceptionally well-placed to serve. Traditionally, the discipline of English studies has always defined its terms by creating, and from time to time adjusting, a literary canon, and where it *has* invoked the help of bibliography and textual criticism, it has been to correct and enhance the authority of a particular version of a relatively few canonical texts. And of course the vermiculate scholar-ship of that activity has its own fascination and commands our respect.

But bibliography itself knows no canon. Its terms of reference as a discipline are the whole archive of recorded texts, their production, re-production, dissemination, and their inter-textual relations. Our short-title catalogues are the tribute we pay to our society's perennial interest in its past. But they are also the most valuable resource we have for the comprehensive reconstruction of our own culture. If we see them in that way, then all past losses reduce our hope of fuller knowledge. By the same token, any prior selection of what it is acceptable or expedient to retain as the nation's archive can only in time distort our understanding of the past and pervert its application in the present. To make that point more precisely: historians and critics who now wish to resurrect marginal texts and their makers (the documents and writers who have always been excluded from the merely literary canon), have their greatest ally in bibliography. If a document was printed, and survives, we can in most cases recover it from Pollard and Redgrave, from Wing, and in due course from the eighteenth- and nineteenth-century short-title catalogues. These will in time become a single archive, searchable throughout at speed and low cost for author, subject, different editions, chronology, and location. When we have such a unified record, it will transform the study of our history, and in particular thereby the study of all who were kept from the centres of power by reason of their sex, race, religion, and their provincial or colonial status. It will enrich the study of any text in its full inter-textual setting, and the study of all versions of that text as new responses to social change. As Nestor says in Shakespeare's *Troilus and Cressida*:

> in such indexes, although small prickes
> To their subsequent volumes, there is seen
> The baby figure of the giant mass
> Of things to come at large.

What we cannot easily do at the moment, however, is construct a model to show the full complexity of text production at any one time. It is simple enough to take a single text and to document its metamorphoses. One might do the same for an author, a bookseller, or a printing house, again with relative ease. The real difficulty lies in reporting on those more limited products and processes in the rich diversity of their relationships one to another, to offer in short a synchronic, not to say 'cohesive', account. Almost all texts of any consequence are the product of the concurrent inter-action of ideologies and institutions, of writers, publishers, printers, binders, wholesalers, travellers, retailers, as well as of the material sources (and their makers and suppliers) of type, paper, cord, and all the appurtenances of a printing house. We, like their writers, habitually think of texts as literary, and therefore either as discrete, as an oeuvre, or as a canon. Most booksellers in the seventeenth century, by contrast, would have thought of their stocks as a range of investments, or as a list of artefacts for sale. A printer almost certainly valued his books and ephemera only as a succession of income-earning jobs. Where the main participants themselves each posited a different interest in the product, and where their labour to produce it was so differently organised by each of them, the achievement of any synthesis true to all may prove to be an impossible ideal.

Still, if we posit as the point of our inquiry the creation of a model, however imperfect, then we might at least begin by recording all we *can* know of a year, a month, a week, a natural day, so that we can start exploring not just the products themselves but the full dynamics of their production and reception in their human and institutional relations.

With that aim in mind, I chose to focus on one year — 1644. In a sense, the date was quite arbitrary, and for purposes of the exercise it would not really matter which year one took. Nevertheless, it is not without a certain felicity. Mr William Sessions reminds me that, as the year of Marston Moor, 1644 was a crucial one for the history of printing in York. First, the royalist printer Stephen Bulkley, who had left London hurriedly in 1642 to overlap briefly with the king and his official travelling printers in York, stopped printing there with the Marston Moor defeat. Second, by autumn 1644, the London-trained parliamentary printer Thomas Broad had arrived in York to begin a business which continued through his widow for over twenty years. In that way, and in microcosm as it were, York provides an image of a time of transition, of the passage from one dispensation to another. But 1644 was also the year in which Milton published, on 5 June, his letter 'Of Education' to Samuel Hartlib, and, on 23 November, *Areopagitica,* his plea for the liberty of unlicensed printing.

My remarks on this occasion, however, are not limited to 1644 but address a range of interests which bear, I think, on several problems in literary and historical research. The topics I have in mind are the scale of text production; the economics of trade; attitudes to print; and the realities of censorship. I shall keep returning to 1644, but I shall also, for comparative purposes, refer to examples from other years.

I begin with statistics. These are boring in their detail but fascinating in their implications. The detail, with the qualifications there noted, is given in the Appendix (on p. 152 infra). It does, I think, require us to modify the inferences drawn by some historians of the period, and suggests in particular the limitations of the Thomason collection as their primary source. Dr Christopher Hill, for example, illustrates as follows an increase in the number of books published in the 1640s: 'Milton's friend the bookseller George Thomason tried to buy a copy of every book and pamphlet published during these exciting times. In 1640 he purchased twenty-two titles; in 1642, one thousand nine hundred and sixty-six. This rate of publication was maintained for the next decade'.[1] As it happens, Dr Hill's equation of a rate of publication with one of acquisition, states my own ideal of copyright deposit; but it was certainly not achieved by Thomason. The wording of the third sentence is also curiously ambiguous. (I assume it does not mean that such a *rate of increase* was maintained for the next decade: a growth from twenty-two to one thousand nine hundred and sixty-six in three years would give an output in 1652 of something like three and a half billion titles.) But even accepting the probable meaning — that publication continued for the next decade at the high level set in 1642 — it would still not be true. Excluding serials, the number of titles extant for 1642 is not one thousand nine hundred and sixty-six but actually about two thousand nine hundred and sixty-eight; it drops to half that for the next year; even lower for 1644; it is under a thousand for 1645; and only once again before 1685 (in 1660) does it even touch two thousand.

Because of its chronological arrangement, the Thomason catalogue, not Wing, is the main source of evidence used by historians for the scale of publication in the years from 1641 to 1660. Yet for all its splendid detail, it is no guide to total production. In 1644, for example, Thomason collected only six hundred and ninety-nine, or about sixty-three per cent, of the one thousand one hundred and thirteen tracts known to be still extant. But even the total number of titles derived from Wing for that one year gives us only the minimum level of production. Excluding serials, but including later editions of the same title, Wing has about seventy thousand entries in all for the years 1641 to 1700. We can only guess the proportion that represents of the total output of the trade, but I suspect that it is not even sixty to seventy per cent of the titles and editions actually published. And if production *was* thirty to forty per cent higher than the entries in Wing suggest, then Thomason may give us less than half the story.

Again, however, evidence is elusive. We find the odd reference to books which seem not to have survived, and there are some lists by authors of the books they say they printed and published but which

1. 'Censorship and English Literature', in *The Collected Essays of Christopher Hill*, 2 vols (Brighton: Harvester Press, 1985), I, p. 40.

are unknown to Wing. A collection of some one thousand five hundred pamphlets recently acquired by Cambridge University Library and all dated between 1660 and 1695, includes some two hundred not traced in Wing. Title-page edition statements are notoriously unreliable, but they too tell us something of what we have lost. Michael Sparke's *Crums of Comfort* survives in only seven of the twenty editions published up to 1635; as Wing lists only the forty-first and forty-second editions, another twenty have disappeared without trace.

So, when we come back to 1644, and any other year for which figures are given, we need to acknowledge the partial nature of the extant archive and be particularly cautious in attributing causes to the patterns of production throughout the century.

Sir Keith Thomas puts, I believe, a point of view commonly accepted by historians when he writes: 'In the 1640s, with the Civil War, all controls seemed to have lapsed altogether and the result was an extraordinary output of heterodox ideas of a kind which would not have been allowed before or afterwards. But normally the system of state licensing, which lasted until the end of the seventeenth century, had a deeply inhibiting effect on publication.'[2]

No one, I think it is fair to say, yet knows if that was so. In fact, it is impossible yet to say if the volume of production actually rose — as measured, for example, by the number of sheets in each book and the number of copies printed of each. At a guess, for my survey is not complete, perhaps half the items printed in 1644 were only single sheets, and at least as many again of those must have been lost, for as a class of ephemera they were the most vulnerable to extinction. Certainly there were more brief pamphlets and fewer substantial books. And although it is true that the number of extant *titles* rises sharply in 1642, witnessing to an increase in the reporting and exchange of opinions in print, one result of a systematic survey is to suggest that few in relation to the whole were heterodox. Indeed, many of the effects claimed for the lapse of licensing in 1641 are largely illusory; but this is a point to which I shall return.

In at least two other ways, the kind of annual surveys of book production I have suggested may help to refine our knowledge of

2. 'The Meaning of Literacy in Early Modern England', in *The Written Word: Literacy in Transition*, edited by Gerd Baumann (Oxford: The Clarendon Press, 1986), p. 120.

the trade, and therefore of the past. One is better knowledge of the incidence of anonymous publication, as measured by the absence of the name or initials of an author, printer or bookseller. The other is printing for the author. Their attendant bibliographical signs are often read as evidence of the influence of censorship. Yet they may be read more correctly, I think, as a normal expression of the general pattern of trade.

The extent to which authors concealed their identity — or simply failed to mention their names in print — is not easy to assess, mainly because we are dependent, at least to begin with, on the form of the Wing attributions and the often ambiguous use of square brackets when authorship is only inferred. Nor does Wing always allow for internal declarations of authorship as distinct from title-page statements. I can say something, however, of the pattern shown by books published in 1644 and, for comparison, 1688. In each case, I assume that the presence of an author's, printer's or bookseller's initials in a work is a declaration of identity. I.M. or J.M., for example, can scarcely be read in the 1640s or the 1660s as a serious attempt by Milton to conceal his authorship. One might have been tempted to think that the title page of one of the 1644 divorce tracts, *The Judgement of Martin Bucer,* had been set in code, for the 'I' and the 'M' of 'IVDGEMENT' are much larger and stand out from the other letters; but Milton gives his full name on B4v. So too the 1644 edition of *The Doctrine and Discipline of Divorce* gives only J.M. on the title page but John Milton in full on A4v.

Again excluding serials, and any work in which we find either an author's name or initials, it is clear that anonymity is far more frequent than not. In 1644, authorship is acknowledged in only four hundred and thirty-six — or forty per cent — of the one thousand one hundred and thirteen items now extant. The figure for 1688 is remarkably consistent at forty-three per cent. Since very few of them could possibly have been influenced by censorship, what we have here is simply the perpetuation of a long-established convention of authors taking a low profile in making their thoughts public. Even as late as 1699, Dryden could write of a revival of Congreve's *Double Dealer* that 'the printing an Authors name, in a Play bill, is a new manner of proceeding, at least in England'.

The convention of anonymity for authors extends to printers, and — more surprisingly — even to booksellers. In 1644, only forty-six per cent of the items published carry a printer's name; and only thirty-two per cent a booksellers' name. For 1688, the figures are thirty-one per cent for printers and thirty-nine per cent for booksellers. Again, it is initially tempting to think that such anonymity in the trade betrays a wish to avoid detection. Did Samuel Simmons leave his name off the first two issues of *Paradise Lost* because of his fear of authority? I think not. If we look at the range of books involved, very few had any reason to conceal their origins. That applies even to those books which give neither a printer nor a bookseller: some twenty-two per cent of the 1644 items, and thirty per cent of those for 1688.

There is nothing sinister in any of this. Nor is there, I think, in the low incidence of entries in the Stationers' Register, notwithstanding the legal obligation to make them. In 1644, only twenty per cent of the books and pamphlets were entered; in 1688, only seven per cent. That decline by 1688 reflects changes in the way booksellers had come to hold and to share their copyrights. The entries for 1644 tell a different story, and again the explanation is more likely to be economic than political: a function of the increase in the number of titles published and a reduction in their length. Very few were likely to be pirated or run to a second edition. Spending 6d. to establish copyright by entry would not therefore have bought any protection worth paying for.

Those comments suggest how events now read as political may actually express straightforward conditions of trade. So too, in many cases, not the threat of reprisal but the costs of printing, inhibited some authors from venturing into print and left them content to circulate their work in manuscript. Richard Williams did not print his book, 'A poore mans pittance', consisting of tracts on Essex and the Gunpowder plot: 'I did pretende to haue put the same in printe and had gotten it lycensed accordinge to order. But a printer asked me a some of moneye for the impression whiche I was not able to paye and so I kepte it privatt.'[3]

When, by contrast, the printer Samuel Simmons agreed to make Milton three successive payments for *Paradise Lost*, Milton may well have been more fortunate than we are accustomed to think. The commoner situation mid-century for many classes of text, including poetry, was more like that of Richard Williams. Were we to know more about the extent of printing at the author's expense, we should

---

3. British Library MS Arundel 418, f. 24^r. I am grateful to Dr J. K. Moore for this reference.

be better able to judge why some works never reached print and why those that did may often be found with such bare imprints as 'Printed in the Year 1644'. The eccentric Lady Eleanor Audeley, or Davies, or Douglas — the same woman: she was much married — has sixty-one items in STC and Wing, but all except two are devoid of any mention of a bookseller or printer. Of the fifty-eight Wing items attributed to her, twenty-seven are anonymous. What we have here is almost certainly a case of books printed for the author: she bore all the costs, and neither printer nor bookseller (if there was one) saw any reason to be named. But, again, there was nothing sinister in their absence from such an imprint.

That solution was also, for some authors, a preferred alternative to the forms of aristocratic patronage common both earlier and later in the century. In 1644 the very idea of patronage was anathema to many. One can see something of feelings on the matter in comments that year by Richard Vines and Francis Quarles. In his book, *The Impostures of Seducing Teachers Discovered,* Vines writes, for example, *'AN Epistle Dedicatory usually bespeakes a Patron, and then the Reader is epistled afterward. I intreat Readers only and Patrons no further than the Truth may challenge them . . .'.* When Cornelius Burges was attacked for dedicating a book to the Earl of Pembroke, a practice described by his critic as *'a meer Popish* Ceremony', Quarles came to his defence in *The Whipper Whipt* with an etymological argument that no subservience was implied by a 'dedication' but only a free act of presentation.[4]

But for many in the 1640s the very acceptance of print as a medium still remained problematic. Writing of literacy in early modern England, Sir Keith Thomas remarked that 'Early modern England . . . was not an oral society. But neither was it a fully literate one . . . it is the interaction between contrasting forms of culture, literate and illiterate, oral and written, which gives this period its particular fascination'.[5]

The reminder is timely, for a phrase like 'the impact of print' — however carefully it is qualified — cannot help but imply a major displacement of writing. In the same way, too great a preoccupation with writing and printing (as the technologies of literacy) may lead us to forget the superior virtues of speech.

As we know, an important difference between talking and writing

4. For Richard Vines, see Wing V557; for Francis Quarles, Wing Q121.
5. 'The Meaning of Literacy in Early Modern England', p. 98.

is what is now called 'presence'. The spoken text can be more sharply defined, and its authority enhanced, by the speaker's control of tone, nuance, gesture, and responsiveness to an audience. Hence for many, happier in the one medium, the dual pressure to speak *and* to publish or to listen *and* to read created problems of choice and adjustment.

Looking for first-hand evidence of those problems, we find it in the ephemeral world of seventeenth-century sermons, topical pamphlets, and serials. It is there that we get our clearest view both of the anxieties created by print and of the possibilities opened up by it. Almost every printed sermon in the first half of the century has something to say by way of apology for the loss of the preacher's presence. 'I know well that *the same* Sermon, *as to the life of it,* is scarcely *the same* in the *hearing,* and in the *reading* . . .', wrote John Ward in 1645. So too, in 1644, Peter Smith had feared that his printed sermon would *'want that little life it seem'd to have when it was utter'd* viva voce, *and entertained with your chearfull and religious attention'*. But these reluctant writers also had to acknowledge some advantages. So again Peter Smith, after quoting Romans to the effect that faith comes by preaching, nevertheless concedes that *'memory is frail; and to reflect again, by reading, upon that wch we have heard, may conduce much unto the improvement of your knowledge'*. Christopher Tesdale, also in 1644, says to his readers: *'I shall bee your remembrancer by restoring the losse of the eare to the eye: Words, we say, are wind, and unless they be taken upon the wing, even while they are flying, and brought to the Presse, they are gone and lost'.*[6]

Others express their concern with the psychology of knowledge in relation to the forms in which it is communicated: *'What the* Pulpit *sent to some of your* eares, *the* Presse *now sends to some of your* eyes; *the good God send it into every one of your* hearts, *into your hands, and lives; the* Argument *is worthy of your eares, eyes, hearts, and hands* . . .', wrote Edmund Staunton in 1644, self-conscious still about turning speech into print and doubtful of its ability to enter the heart. Dr John Strickland, the same year: the words *'have been already in your eares, they are now before your eyes, the Lord write them into our hearts, that we may be doers of the word, and not hearers only* . . .'.[7] What is revealing about these unprofound

6. For Peter Smith, see Wing S4142; for Christopher Tesdale, Wing T792; for John Ward, Wing W773.

7. For Edmund Staunton, see Wing S5342; for John Strickland, Wing S5969.

comments is their frequency, their self-consciousness, and their still tentative, uncertain quality.

Concern and regret, if not quite the same anxiety, may also be found at the gradual shift from oral to written pleading in the law courts. Under the system of oral pleading, the forms were settled only after exhaustive debate in court, with all the opportunities it provided for clarification and correction. Then, when the pleadings were enrolled, they were accurate. By contrast, written pleadings, whose terms were settled by the parties out of court, were open to error. Hale, for example, in his *History of the Common Law Pleas of the Crown,* thought the oral evidence at common law far superior to the written evidence in courts of equity, because it is delivered 'personally, and not in writing; [in writing] often time, yea too often, a crafty clerk, commissioner or examiner, will make a witness speak what he truly never meant by dressing it up in his own terms, phrase and expressions. Whereas on the other hand, many times the very *manner* of delivering testimony, will give a probable indication, whether the witness speaks truly or falsely. And by this means also he has an opportunity to correct, amend or explain his testimony, upon further questioning with him; which he can never have, after a deposition is set down in writing.'[8] That is a good description of the virtues of speech as presence. The paradox of writing – that what seems *exact* when first written can be torn a thousand ways by critical reading – led Francis Bacon to resist the reduction of common law to statute form. As he said in 1616, 'there are more doubts that arise upon our statutes, which are a text law, than upon the common law, which is no text law'.[9] To bring words on a page up to date, we must either strain their meaning, or revise and reprint them.

The powerful myth of the permanence of print – the art that preserves all arts – is only part of the story. What we need equally to stress, I think, is the ephemerality of much that is printed. To do so would at least help us to see more readily certain affinities it still had, in the minds of many at this time, with speech.

When we look at the books themselves, we can see writers and printers seeking to limit the difference of print by devising ways to

8. Sir Matthew Hale, *History of the Common Law* (1713), second edition corrected (1716), cited by W. S. Holdsworth, *A History of English Law*, 16 vols (1922–66), VI, p. 592.

9. Cited by J. H. Baker, *An Introduction to English Legal History,* second edition (London: Butterworths, 1979), p. 189.

suggest its affinities with speaking and writing. It is most notable of course in forms of address and of dialogue; and it is one of the important uses of marginal notes.

So, Milton would speak in print: 'They who, to States and Governors of the Commonwealth direct their *Speech,* High Court of Parliament, or wanting such access in a private condition, write that which they forsee may advance the public good . . .'. As a rhetorical strategy, *Areopagitica, a Speech . . . To the Parliament of England,* assumes an oral condition. By adopting such a form, Milton becomes present to the Commons. And yet his pamphlet is clearly written to be read, not heard. The amphibolous state of that 'speech' or 'pamphlet' is shared in part by Milton's other addresses to Parliament at that time printed in *The Doctrine and Discipline of Divorce* and *Tetrachordon.* And when we come to the letter (or should it be *tract?*), 'Of Education', we see Milton exploiting yet another interstitial space. Is this a private letter made public print ('Thus Master *Hartlib,* you have a generall view in writing of that which I had severall times discourst with you . . .'); or is it really conceived as a text to be printed which merely exploits the fiction of being a private communication? Milton moves easily and positively into the double role of speaker and writer; yet his fluency in speech, manuscript and print is not just a mark of his peculiar genius but a skill demanded by his times if he was to reach all members of his commonwealth. Writing of toleration in 1673, in his little tract *Of True Religion,* he holds that Protestants should be able 'on all occasions to give account of their Faith . . . by Arguing, Preaching in their several Assemblies, Publick writing, and the freedom of Printing'. In other words, in each and every mode.

The development in print of different registers to signal that variety of forms is one of the fascinating features of the book trade at this time. Milton's words 'Publick writing' are exactly right for his own sense of address. This practice of using print more generally as if it *were* a public speaking and writing is found at its most efficient in the informal genres of ephemera, the small pamphlet, and the printed speech. There is a form of communicative interchange here, the extent of which would, I think, be hard to parallel in the years immediately before or after the seventeenth century.

It is quite remarkable, for example, how many texts imply some kind of direct address or dialogue. Milton's *Colasterion* is 'A reply to a nameless answer against . . .' *The Doctrine and Discipline of Divorce.*

Wing lists four hundred and twenty-four titles which begin in the form 'An Answer to'. Another five hundred and sixty-two begin as titles of address in the form 'To the . . .'. 'Humble' addresses, desires, hints, petitions, propositions, remonstrances, representations, requests, supplications, and so on, account for another three hundred and twenty-seven. Petitions, proposals and propositions (the ones which do not begin as 'Humble') number three hundred and seventeen. 'His Majesty' answers, declares or sends messages to another thirty. Titles beginning with the words Animadversion, Answer, Antidote, Confutation, Dialogue (one hundred and fifty-three of those), Reflection, Refutation, Remarks, Reply, Response, Vindication, Voice and Vox, altogether number six hundred and eighty-two. 'A Letter' or 'Letters to' account for eight hundred and two items. The round total they make is at least three thousand one hundred and forty-four. That figure, moreover, excludes all separate-issues and re-issues and reprintings, and (with the sole exception of His Majesty) it also *ex*cludes every comparable item entered under or cross-referenced to an author's name. A quick test of how many more might be involved were we to include those classes may be made by taking the title entries for 'Vindication'. Only seventy-eight were included in the above calculations, but there are in fact one hundred and ninety-nine such entries, or two and a half times as many again. This interchange of highly topical texts, of short pamphlets with short lives, helped to break down the anxiety-provoking distinctions between speech, manuscript and print, and to confirm the use of printing in its ephemeral uses.

Printing is of course much inferior to speech when it comes to conveying the spatial dynamics of speaker and audience, but what is fascinating to observe in the 1644 books is the skill with which printers tried to 'set forth' in their own terms at least something of the social space of dialogue. Where the extensions of dialogue are most notable is in the inter-textual levels so many pamphlets present. This may be done by the alternation of texts and counter-texts. So Quarles, in his defence of Cornelius Burges, adopts a kind of typographic drama: the biblical David presents the text of Burges; Calumniator, son of Nimshi (a great worshipper of calves), speaks the text of Burges's critics; and Quarles's own text is given to Jonathan as The Replyer. Paragraph by paragraph throughout the book they take their turn in the debate.[10] In Cheynell's attack on Chillingworth,

10. *The Whipper Whipt* (1644), Wing Q121.

the questions are set up in italic, Chillingworth's answers in black letter, and Cheynell's comments in roman.[11] In *A Vindication of Episcopacie,* the pamphlet under attack is reprinted and then demolished, a paragraph at a time, for the entire book. We find the same thing in *The Cavaliers New Common-prayer Booke Vnclasp't,* first printed at York in 1644. This too is entirely reprinted in London 'with some brief and necessary *Observations,* to refute the Lyes and Scandalls that are contained in it'. These observations are interposed in smaller type between the paragraphs. When they fail to serve, qualifications, assertions, rebuttals, imputed meanings, all set in italic and put in square brackets, invade the main text itself. One of the neatest pieces of inter-textual presentation in the period is *A Solemn League and Covenant,* both as it was agreed at Westminster and then as modified in Edinburgh. It gives the Westminster text, but as one edition notes: '*The several additions to the Scottish forme are here printed in a different letter*' [namely, italics within square brackets] and '*The omissions and other alterations are noted in the margent*'.[12]

Marginal notes are one of the best pointers there are to the nature of textual exchange. In their citation of sources, they have an inter-textual function. Milton, of course, could afford to be scathing about any marginal display of erudition. When he was abroad, as he records in *Church Government* (1641), he had 'to club quotations with men whose learning and beleif lies in marginal stuffings . . . and horse-loads of citations'. Others, less confident than he, felt they had to make their excuses if their margins were bare. 'If it trouble thee (Good Reader) to see so bare a margin, so few Authors cited, or this Sermon come abroad in so homely and plaine a dresse . . .', wrote John Shaw in *Brittains Remembrancer,* it is all because his books and papers were plundered a year before; that copies of his sermons were demanded within three days of preaching it; and that '*I had only time* to write it once over, so as the Printer got it from me by pieces of sheets, as it was written (which makes it somewhat more confused) . . .'. Thomas Blake, in *The birth-privilege,* fears that '*Some will complain of a naked Margin, to which much might be said, The Author was with books when it was compiled for the* Pulpit, *but taken from*

11. Francis Cheynell, *Chillingworthi novissima* (1644), Wing C3810.

12. For *A Vindication of Episcopacie,* see Wing V477; for *The Cavaliers New Common-prayer Booke Vnclasp't,* Wing C1578; and for the *Solemn League and Covenant,* see, for example, *A Copie of the Covenant* (1644), Wing C6210.

them when it was fitted for the Presse. *So that use of Marginal References must have put upon him the borrowed copies of others, and a new paines for the quotation of Chapter & Page.'* Even more pertinently, however, he argues that *'the quotations desired must either have been* friends, *and so their Evidence would be challenged; or else* Adversaries, *which perhaps might provoke some personall offences and distaste, which the Authour studiously professeth to avoid'.*[13] Challenge and provocation, so natural in oral debate but so hard to convey in print, are there seen as a function of the marginal note. Under those continuing conditions of uncertainty about the precise status of speech and print, it is not surprising to note the relatively late development (in 1668) of the now familiar distinction between slander and libel.[14] In the 1640s, publishing a libel need not have involved printing it. Consequently the forms of suppression and censure were themselves less straightforward, as well as less severe, than some historians and critics have assumed.

Dr Christopher Hill and Professor Annabel Patterson, for example, have each argued that the censorship seriously inhibited writers, at worst silencing them and at best driving them into a rhetoric of obliquity. We are therefore enjoined, in effect, to study not only the texts that *were* written, but the *un*written ones too: 'certain words, certain ideas, that could not be printed'. As Dr Hill puts it, 'Historians looking only at the words on the page risk entering into an unwritten conspiracy with seventeenth-century censors'.[15] Of course, since such readings depend crucially upon a knowledge of the events and opinions that were suppressed and their relation to the words of the texts as we actually have them, they are not without their risks.

The problem is not just an academic one. Let me enforce the point by telling a slightly chilling story. The two editors of a recent joint edition of the letters of a major writer agreed to divide their labours. One dealt with letters before, the other with letters after, a certain date. Unbeknown to each other, they each edited the same undated letter and supplied it with a convincing set of notes to date it and to

13. For John Shaw, see Wing S3023A; for Thomas Blake, Wing B3142.

14. The essential change may be charted in King v. Lake (1668); see A. Kiralfy, *A Source Book of English Law* (London: Sweet and Maxwell, 1957), pp. 154–63; Baker, op. cit., p. 374; and Holdsworth, op. cit., V. pp. 346–47, 360–61, 364-65.

15. Christopher Hill, 'Censorship and English Literature', pp. 32, 50; and Annabel Patterson, *Censorship and Interpretation* (Madison: University of Wisconsin Press, 1984), passim.

explain the allusions. Each 'edition' was in itself highly plausible, but of course the two were mutually exclusive. Happily, an alert copy-editor averted any public embarrassment. But one can easily see how the nature of language, which leaves a text open, and the density of history, which compels selection, can make for some intoxicating recipes.

There is not space to pursue at proper length on this occasion the topic of censorship, but since one of the most impressive books to appear in 1644 was Milton's *Areopagitica* it demands at least brief comment. One of the things I would wish to stress, by contrast with Dr Hill and Professor Patterson, is the relative inefficiency of control, and to affirm the courage of the writers, printers and booksellers who wrote, printed and dispersed the multitude of unlicensed texts.

The fullest recent discussion I know of seditious libel in the period is that by Philip Hamburger who makes it abundantly clear that 'most so-called seditious libel trials before 1696 were not for the common law offence of libel but . . . for violations of specific licensing statutes . . . or the royal prerogative to license printed books'.[16] Of the options open to government — such as prosecutions for treason, scandalum magnatum, and heresy, all of which carried heavy penalties — the simplest to execute was a system of licensing. When, in 1642, new legislation was being considered to control the press, the judges reported to the Lords that the mere printing of libels was a publication of them, since their printing implied distribution. But the law of libel was thought much more difficult to apply than pre-publication censorship, and when the Order of June 1643 came to be drafted, it therefore settled for licensing as the simpler means of control.

This almost uniform policy of all governments throughout the century to employ licensing laws to prosecute the press is of greatest importance in deciding the extent and seriousness of any infringements. To begin with, all punishments under the Star Chamber decrees of 1586 and 1637 were less severe than those prescribed by other laws. Only at times of greatest danger (1588, 1601, the 1630s, 1649, immediately after the Restoration, and in the 1680s) did government proceed under legislation which allowed the harsher penalties of death or mutilation. Indeed, in the absence of press laws,

16. Philip Hamburger, 'The Development of the Law of Seditious Libel and the Control of the Press', *Stanford Law Journal*, 37 (1984–5), pp. 661–765, esp. p. 674.

there was no lesser course open. It may seem a paradox, but the effect of the licensing laws, when they were in force, was to mitigate the crime. Lilburne's trial in 1638, just after the 1637 decree, was for violating its licensing provisions. Even when the charge *was* treason, it was rarely the testimony of a text which determined the verdict.

Nor did any government find it at all easy to restrain the press. In fact, as Hamburger says, 'the legal and political restraints on [its] ability to deal effectively with the press frequently left the Crown in very straitened legal circumstances'. Finally, 'it had a continual struggle to maintain a legal basis for prosecution [and was] obliged to abandon one law after another as those in use became inadequate, defunct, or otherwise obsolete'.[17] Against Dr Hill's view that 'The ending of ecclesiastical control seems to me the most significant event in the history of seventeenth-century English literature',[18] one must stress Hamburger's view that control by licensing was virtually continuous, and only fitfully efficient, and Holdsworth's successive demonstrations that the abolition of Star Chamber in 1641 changed little.[19]

Indeed, the Star Chamber decrees of 1586 and 1637, like the order of June 1643 and the post-Restoration licensing acts, combined to serve the interests both of government and the book trade. They prescribed the licensing of books to be printed, they ordered the registration of copies, and they gave the Stationers' Company a role in enforcing the provisions. It is important to realise that those provisions were actively sought by the Company as a means of restraining competition, of ensuring (at least in principle) equitable conditions for members of the Company, and to secure the privilege of self-regulation. Licensing was a condition of the registration of copyright, and registration was some defence against piracy. The regulations limiting the number of master printers, presses, apprentices, and the size of editions, like the restriction of printing to London, Oxford and Cambridge, helped to minimise unemployment. The powers of search and seizure conferred upon the Company were economic powers, used as much to stamp out irregular and competitive printing as to serve government interests in the detection of seditious literature. The lapse of licensing provisions in 1641–42

17. Ibid., pp. 760–61.

18. Christopher Hill, 'Censorship and English Literature', p. 40.

19. Holdsworth, op. cit., V, pp. 336, 338–40, 342, 360–61; VIII, pp. 406–07.

removed the Company members' legal protection, and they were reduced to the informal acknowledgement of custom and precedent. There were, for example, no common law rights in copyright. To resecure its ancient rights, and later to have its charter renewed, it was formally requisite for the Company to add its voice to the frequent proclamations against scandalous pamphlets and their dispersers; and yet it was privately possible for any member of the Company to print and disperse such texts if it was in their commercial, personal or ideological interests to do so. Time and again, commerce compromised censorship. While members of the Company may have worked to discover scandalous printing, they also worked to conceal it. So long as the texts involved did not infringe other members' copyrights, or did not figure in the more general trade rivalries between patentees and splinter groups within the Company, there was little reason to fear exposure.

That complicity of the government's interests and those of the trade in the construction of a licensing system, ensured a certain level of routine efficiency, but it also involved some important tolerances. For example, it did not touch manuscripts. It substituted a less serious and often merely technical offence for those previously charged. As a corollary, it displaced harsher penalties by milder ones. As the normal condition of control, it reduced the incidence of more serious charges. When more serious charges were intermittently brought – for treason, scandalum magnatum, or seditious libel – it was less a question of censorship than one of acute political crisis and overt danger to the State. In its routine operations, licensing worked most efficiently for the least contentious texts. Conversely, its irrelevance to uncontentious texts bred a contempt for its procedures. That contempt is also revealed in the enormous output of radically subversive literature under conditions of ostensibly strict control, and the failure of authority to punish those responsible. The Journals of the Lords and Commons, and the State Papers (Domestic), are full of allusions to such unlicensed texts, and to those who wrote, printed or dispersed them – I have extracted all there are for the years 1641 to 1700 – but proof of the offence, and evidence of arrest and punishment, are much more difficult to discover. Where one can find it, there is also enough evidence of mild fines, remission of penalties, merciful release, pardon granted for kneeling at the bar of the House – and sheer recidivism – to suggest that, for all the officially declared concern, infringements of the licensing laws were normally not harshly punished. It is called 'keeping up appearances'.

It is difficult to know what to make of Dr Hill's arguments for the savagery of the Laudian censorship following the decree of 1637, when the claim is also made that 'Apparently 65% of books published in 1640 were unlicensed'.[20] So, the statement that 'The number of authorised printers in London was cut to twenty' is formally true (but several appealed to and were helped by Laud to continue); 'unlicensed printers were to be pilloried and whipped' (but they were not); 'corporal penalties were imposed on those who offended against these decrees, regardless of rank' (but those who offended by not printing the imprimatur went unpunished).[21] Greg has estimated that about one-third of all books published up to 1640 were never entered in the Stationers' Register, and yet that persistent offence against the decrees also went unpunished; and most of the few recorded whippings, brandings, ear-croppings and nose-slittings listed as proof of the harshness of the censorship were for greater and long-established crimes, not for offences against the 1637 or earlier decrees as such.

In 1644 *Areopagitica* was not, I believe, provoked by indignation at the penalties which might be imposed on any who transgressed, nor was it an instant and outraged response to the Order of 1643. What goaded Milton into writing was the irritant of harrassment. The new licensing order against which he writes was published on 14 June 1643. Why did *Areopagitica* not appear until as late as 23 November 1644 (seventeen months later)? Was *Milton* at a loss for words?

The printers most closely associated with Milton throughout his life, from his earliest prose pamphlets to *Paradise Lost* itself, were Matthew Simmons, his wife Mary, and their son Samuel. Matthew Simmons and Thomas Paine were two printers who, it was said in 1641, 'have continually printed libels, are known to all the stationers, and have their press in Red cross Street'.[22] The words 'their press' tell us they ran a single shop in partnership, an association that had its origins in the time they spent together as apprentices in the printing house of John Dawson. Matthew's imprints are among the commonest in 1644 and his involvement with Milton, in particular, was not without excitement.

20. Christopher Hill, 'Censorship and English Literature', p. 49.

21. Ibid., p. 37.

22. *CJ*, II, p. 267.

On 10 July 1644, the Stationers' Company reported two sellers of imported bibles to the Lords; and on 26 August, they petitioned the Commons about the deleterious effects on their own trade of the bible patentees (Matthew Simmons was one of those who signed the petition). But, seeking its quid pro quo, the very same day the Commons asked the Stationers 'diligently to inquire out the Authors, Printers, and Publishers, of the Pamphlet . . . concerning Divorce'.[23] This was almost certainly *The Judgement of Martin Bucer* that Simmons had just printed. It had been licensed and entered at Stationers' Hall on 15 July, well before printing; it was addressed directly to 'The Parlament' by Milton himself (his name is on B4v); it bore Simmons's imprint; and it was in Thomason's hands by 6 August.

It is ironic that it was the reception of this 1644 pamphlet, one that obeyed all the rules for publication, that provoked the writing of *Areopagitica*. Given the delay between the revival of pre-publication licensing in June 1643 and the publication of *Areopagitica* only in November 1644, we must, I think, see its writing as Milton's deeply personal reaction to criticism of his divorce tracts. This came from, among others, Thomas Hill and Herbert Palmer in August 1644 and coincided with the intervention of the Stationers' Company on the same theme at the same time. Milton matched the direct addresses to Parliament by his critics and the Stationers (Hill's and Palmer's were made by sermon, the Stationers' by petition) with a speech of his own. By contrast with that compelling pattern of events, there is simply no sign, in June 1643, of Milton's principled concern, as a writer, at the reimposition of pre-publication censorship.

Two weeks after *Areopagitica* appeared, the Lords asked the Stationers to find out the printer of a 'Libel against the Peerage of this Realm'. They reported back on 28 December that, despite 'their best Endeavours', they had failed to 'make any discovery therefore, the Letter being so common a Letter'. But, needing the Lords' support, they took the chance to complain 'of the frequent Printing of scandalous Books by divers, as *Hezechia Woodward* and *Jo. Milton*'.[24] As a result, the Lords immediately ordered the examination of Woodward and Milton, and any others the Stationers reported. Simmons and Paine had printed both authors. But Simmons went on to produce, initially with Paine, within only a few weeks of

23. *CJ*, III, p. 606.

24. *LJ*, VII, p. 116.

the Lords' demand, a further edition of *The Doctrine and Discipline of Divorce,* and then first editions of Milton's *Colasterion* and the *Tetrachordon,* and almost certainly further books by Hezechiah Woodward.

It all points to a strange mix of irritating but impotent interventions by government and a sturdy refusal by writers and printers to be cowed. A telling example from 1644 of one licenser's attitudes to the system is Charles Herle's comments on Thomas Fuller's *Sermon: Of Reformation.* It was examined and censored by Saltmarsh, and then licensed by Herle in that form. Herle's answer to Fuller's complaint when he discovered the changes nicely reveals how the rules might be bent for the right person. But it is also interesting for what it implies about meaning.

> . . . *I must confesse, had I knowne you to have been the Author* [wrote Herle] *I should have endeavoured to have satisfied M. Saltmarsh of your good meaning therein, before I had set my hand to his Examinations of it. Your other Books made me conceive the Authour some other of your name.*

Then he added:

> [But the sermon] *is not in itselfe so free from some passages that may admit of an ill meaning (at least, had the Authour been such as was reported) . . . My licensing the Examination of some passages of your Sermon, was (at most) but on supposition their meaning had been such as some conceited them, and suppositions are no accusations: you know the rule nihil ponunt ni re, they affirme nothing; nor (had they been accusations) is it but the rule of Parliamentary Iustice, to have heard the Authours sense of his own words, before it condemned him to a prison.*

Those remarks preface the text of a book by Herle himself. He concludes by hoping that none will construe the references to King Ahab and Jezabel in *his* sermon as referring in any way to the Sovereign and his Consort![25]

Fuller, like Milton and Simmons, was one worthy to be Sealed of the Tribe of Ben. In his poem of that name, Jonson wrote:

> Men that are safe, and sure, in all they doe,
> Care not what trials they are put unto;
> They meet the fire, the Test, as Martyrs would;
> And though Opinion stampe them not, are gold.

25. Wing H1551.

It may have been a self-protective strategy for its printer to suppress his name from *Areopagitica*, but Milton had no qualms about boldly declaring his authorship on its title page and daring the Commons to strike back.

The politics of language, the power of texts, the impositions and subversions of authority in every communicative mode, have recently — and I think properly — become a dominant concern of those interested in literature, history and politics. But most of the inquiries into such questions are so focussed on the minutiae of verbal language, or are built on such shaky historical assumptions, that they seriously underestimate, not only the courage of writers, but the material conditions of production, the varieties of labour, the economics of trade, and their dominance in text production. These are conditions of such variety and complexity that no single historical explanation, like censorship, can be seen as so fully determinative. However sympathetic one must be to those oppressed at any time by censorship, and however disposed — as I am myself — to resent its revival in our own society, we cannot, as bibliographers, historians or critics, altogether free ourselves from certain laws of evidence, certain historical constraints on interpretation. To do otherwise, is to risk creating false assumptions about past writers' attitudes to, for example, print and censorship, and about their forms of response.

I have tried to sketch some of the material and other conditions which affected the ways in which texts were produced and disseminated in the mid-1640s. My evidence has been drawn almost entirely from the book trade and may be broadly described as bibliographical. To return to my opening remarks: if we are to move forward *'Ad correctionem'* and *'ad aedificandum'*, whether as literary, political, or social historians, we shall do so the more certainly, I venture to suggest, if we also recognise the importance of historical bibliography as the foundation of our enterprise.

APPENDIX

Wing Statistics for Calendar Years 1644 and 1688

Books, etc.

		1644		1688	
Total items so dated or attributed by Wing to those years (excludes serials)		1113		1519	
London-printed:	named printers	324		347	
	no printer named	533	857	945	1292
Non-London-printed:	named printers	175		115	
	no printer named	66	241	74	189
Foreign-printed:	named printers	10		15	
	no printer named	5	15	23	38
All areas:	no printer *or* bookseller named	247		455	
Total items:	named printers	509		477	
	no printer named	604		1042	

Serials

		1644		1688	
Number of titles (Nelson and Seccombe)		37		23	
Number of issues		684		445+	
Thomason Tracts		699		—	
Term Catalogues		—		242	
Stationers' Regr Entries —	Books	231		101	
	Serials	417	648	—	
Printing for Parliament —	Extant	155			
(Lambert)	Not found	53	208	—	

Wing items for 1641–9 (calendar years) as listed in Lambert, *Printing for Parliament, 1641–1700*. Those for 1649–84 are for old-style years (1649/50–1684/5) and are rounded to the nearest 25 from the graph given by Mason, *The Library* (June 1974). The figures exclude serials.

1641	1642	1643	1644	1645	1646	1647	1648	1649
1850	2968	1495	1020	978	1049	1488	1826	1250

1650	1651	1652	1653	1654	1655	1656	1657	1658
1025	875	925	1075	925	1000	975	950	975

1659	1660	1661	1662	1663	1664	1665	1666	1667
1725	2175	1250	1125	800	675	725	475	525

1668	1669	1670	1671	1672	1673	1674	1675	1676
625	600	850	700	850	825	875	1000	900

1677	1678	1679	1680	1681	1682	1683	1684	
800	950	1350	1775	1575	1475	1425	1425	

Index

Horne, H. P., early work on bookbinding (1894), 31.
Howarth, R. G., ed. Pepys's letters, 112.
Howe, Ellic, on London bookbinders, 38.
Hume, David, dependent upon William Strahan, printer, 5; compares Strahan to Aldus, Reuchlin, and 'Stevens' (Estienne?), 6.
Huntington, Henry E., as book collector, 121.
Hyde, Mary, as book collector, 121.

Insobriety and bookbinding, connection between, 43.

Johnson Samuel, his love of books, 87; *Rambler* No. 92, 88; to Mrs Thrale, 88; *Rambler* No. 57, 89; *Dictionary of the English Language*, 91, 97–99; quoted, 100–01; Idler essay No. 91, 100; Idler essay No. 85, 102; Idler essay No. 51, 102.
Jones, John Paul, of Galloway, 'father' of U.S. Navy, 69.
Jonson, Ben, quoted, 131, 150.

Keith, George, tenth Earl Marischal, 70.
Keith, James, Field-Marshal, Governor of Berlin, 70.
Ker, Neil, on an unpublished panel stamp, 43; his book on pastedowns, 43.
Keynes, Sir Geoffrey, *see* Goldschmidt.
King's Binder, 36.
King, Walker, Bishop of Rochester, literary executor (with French Laurence) of Edmund Burke, 12–14.

Lamb, Charles, on Coleridge as a borrower of books, 87.
Langford, Paul, ed. *inter alios*, of works of Edmund Burke, 11.
Laud, Archbishop, as book collector, 121-22; censorship, 148.
Laurence, French, literary executor (with Walker King) of Edmund Burke, 12-14.
Lauriston, Comte de, *see* Law, James.
Law, James (1768—1828), Comte de Lauriston, Marshal of France, 70.
Law, John, of Lauriston (1671—1729), founder of Banque Général, career, 70.
Law, William, Colonel in Austrian regiment, 70.
Lee, Sir Sidney, ed. *Dictionary of National Biography*, 68.
Leighton, Archibald, binder mainly responsible for development of binding in calico, 45.
Leighton, Douglas, on machine casing, and binding fabric, 45.
Leipzig Book Fair, 59.
Leroy, Jules, author of *l'Éthiopie Archéologie et culture* (1973), 29.
Lewis, Charles, leader of London bookbinders in the 1820s and 1830s, 39.
Library (The), articles on bookbinding in, by: H. J. B. Clements on armorial book stamps (1939), 33; G. D. Hobson on Romanesque bindings (1934—35, 1938—39), 35; Graham Pollard on changes of styles in binding (1956), on construction (1962), and on fifteenth-century binders (1970), 37; I. G. Philip on Roger Bartlett (1955), 43; W. O. Hassell on Sir Christopher Hatton's bindings (1950), 42; Howard Nixon on Bartlett (1962), 42; Giles Barber on centre- and corner-piece bindings (1962), 42, and on Richard Dymott (1964), 42; R. J. Roberts on Sir Christopher Hatton's book stamps (1975), 42; Sir Robert Birley on bindings in Eton College Library (1956), and on Roger and Thomas Payne (1960), 43; William S. Mitchell on James Fleming (1960), 43; Neil Ker on an unpublished panel stamp (1962), 43; Bernard Middleton ed. of broadside about the processes of binding (1962), 45; Douglas Leighton on binding fabric (1948), 45.
Libri, Guglielmo, mid-nineteenth-century book-thief, 31.
Literature of English Bookbinding (The), *see* Bookbindings.